ACTS OF WORSHIP FOR ASSEMBLIES
VOLUME 3

By the same author:
Acts of Worship for Assemblies
Acts of Worship for Assemblies Volume 2
Assemblies for School and Children's Church
Assembly Themes
The Legend of the Fourth Wise Man
More Assembly Services
A Pocket Guide to the Anglican Church
Services for Betweenagers

ACTS OF WORSHIP FOR ASSEMBLIES
Volume 3

by

R. H. LLOYD

Precentor of Christ Church Cathedral, Oxford
formerly Chaplain of the Dragon School, Oxford

MOWBRAY
LONDON & OXFORD

ISBN 0 264 67108 2

First published 1986
by A. R. Mowbray & Co. Ltd,
Saint Thomas House, Becket Street,
Oxford, OX1 1SJ

Typeset by Acorn Bookwork, Salisbury, Wiltshire
Printed in Great Britain by Biddles Ltd, Guildford

British Library Cataloguing in Publication Data

Lloyd, R. H.
Acts of worship for assemblies.
Vol. 3
1. Schools—Exercises and recreations
2. Schools—Prayers
I. Title
377′.1 BV283.S3

ISBN 0-264-67108-2

To: The Revd Craufurd Murray, Vicar of Upper Hutt, New Zealand,
without whose generous contribution this book
would not have seen the light of day.

ACKNOWLEDGEMENTS

The Author and Publisher have made every effort in their requests for permissions to reproduce passages and apologize for any inadvertent omissions. They wish specifically to acknowledge the following:

Cambridge University Press for permission to quote from the N.E.B.

New Zealand Times

LYNDA JONES

BRIAN BOOBBYER

WILLIAM BARCLAY, *Epilogues & Prayers*, S.C.M. Press

WILLIAM BARCLAY, *In the Hands of God*. Collins Fount Paperbacks
World Christian Digest 1948 & 1950

IAN SHEVILL, *Going it – with God*.

YERGENY YERTUSHENKO, *A Precocious Autobiography*. Penguin Books.

LEWIS DAVIES

RICHARD FROST

JANET M. HUINS

ROY COLLINS

T. H. WHITE. *The Once and Future King*. Fontana/Collins 1981

LEWIS THOMAS. *Seven Wonders of My World*. Readers Digest June 1984

ARNOLD LOBEL. *Owl at Home*. World's Work Ltd. The Windmill Press, Kingswood, Tadworth, Surrey.

J. H. SHEPHERD, Christ Church, Oxford.

F. V. EMERY, St Peter's College, Oxford.

J. G. WILLIAMS

CRAUFURD MURRAY, Upper Hutt, New Zealand.

D. P. DEVITT, The Dragon School, Oxford.

CHARLES DILLEY

CONTENTS

PREFACE

Those of us who are privileged to lead people in worship must aim at making them aware of the presence of God. We must assure them that the God whom we worship is there to listen and to help, that God cares, and that God answers our prayers. We must assure them that God has the power to help. After all, there would be little point in praying to a God who is as powerless to deal with life as we are! We must try to make them realize that the God whom we worship is not simply pure Spirit, but that he has the face of Jesus of Nazareth, and that is why we can be certain of his availability, of his love, of his wisdom and of his power.

Christ Church, Oxford, 1986 R. H. LLOYD

Go forth upon your ways in peace:
Be of good courage:
Hold fast that which is good:
Render to no man evil for evil:
Strengthen the faint-hearted:
Support the weak:
Help the afflicted:
Honour all men:
Love and serve the Lord,
Rejoicing in the power of the Holy Spirit.

And the blessing of God Almighty, the Father, the Son and the Holy Spirit, be upon you and remain with you always.

1

RELIGION

Aim: Men will wrangle for religion; write for it; fight for it; die for it; anything but – live it.

(*Colton*)

No doubt religion has to answer for some of the most terrible crimes in history. But that is the fault not of religion but of the ungovernable brute in man.

(*Mahatma Gandhi*)

Illustration:
A rabbi and a soapmaker went for a walk together. The soapmaker said, 'What good is religion? Look at the trouble and misery in the world after thousands of years of religion. If religion is true, why should this be?'

The rabbi said nothing. They continued walking until he noticed a child, filthy with mud and grime, playing in the gutter. The rabbi said, 'Look at that child. You say that soap makes people clean. We've had soap for generations yet look how dirty that child is. Of what value is soap?'

The soapmaker protested, 'But Rabbi, soap can't do any good unless it is used!'

'Exactly', replied the rabbi.

READINGS:

1 Timothy 6,6–19. 'They think religion should yield dividends; and of course religion does yield high dividends, but only to the man whose resources are within him. We brought nothing into the world, because when we leave it we cannot take anything with us either, but if we have food and covering we may rest content. Those who want to be rich fall into temptations and snares and many foolish harmful desires which plunge men into ruin and perdition. The love of money is the root of all evil things, and there are some who in reaching for it have wandered from the faith and spiked themselves on many thorny griefs.

But you, man of God, must shun all this, and pursue justice, piety, fidelity, love, fortitude, and gentleness. Run the great race of faith and take hold of eternal life. For to this you were called; and you confessed your faith nobly before many witnesses. Now in the presence of God, who gives life to all things, and of Jesus Christ, who himself made the same noble confession and gave his testimony to it before Pontius Pilate, I charge you to obey your orders irreproachably and without fault until our Lord Jesus Christ appears. That appearance God will bring to pass in his own good time – God who in eternal felicity alone holds sway. He is King of kings and Lord of lords; he alone possesses immortality, dwelling in unapproachable light. No man has ever seen or ever can see him. To him be honour and might for ever. Amen.)

Instruct those who are rich in this world's goods not to be proud, and not to fix their hopes on so uncertain a thing as money, but upon God, who endows us richly with all things to enjoy. Tell them to hoard a wealth of noble actions by doing good, to be ready to give away and to share, and so acquire a treasure which will form a good foundation for the future. Thus they will grasp the life which is life indeed.'

St Matthew 5,1–12.

Ephesians 4,26–32.

PRAYERS:

O Lord, open our eyes to see what is beautiful;
Our minds, to know what is true,
Our hearts to love what is good;
For Jesus sake. *Amen*.

O Lord, give us more love, more self denial, more likeness to thee. Teach us to sacrifice our comforts to others, and our likings for the sake of doing good. Make us kindly in thought, gentle in word, generous in deed. Teach us that it is better to give than to receive, better to forget ourselves than to put ourselves forward; better to minister than to be ministered unto. And unto thee, the God of Love, be all glory and praise both now and for evermore. *Amen*.

(*Dean Alford*)

HYMNS: *Our blest Redeemer, ere he breathed*
O thou not made with hands

2

2

CRISIS

Aim: If we learn to use adversity positively it can frequently lead to the discovery of the potential which lies within us all.

The north wind made the Vikings.

Illustration:
The largest cut diamond in the world is to be found mounted in the British Imperial Sceptre and is called *the* Cullinan or as it is more popularly known 'The Great Star of Africa'. It was discovered in South Africa in 1905 in a mine some three hundred miles north east of Kimberley and sent to Amsterdam to be cut by a man called Asscher who was the finest lapidarist of his day. Asscher spent three years carefully marking it. When he was satisfied that his preparations were complete, he cut a notch in the great stone. Next, he placed the edge of a special cleaver in the notch, and, carefully raising his metal gavel, he struck a blow. Such was the precision of the blow, it caused the large diamond to cleave in two, thereby releasing two perfect diamonds, which are unexcelled in cut, clarity and colour. The smaller of the two was named Cullinan II and is to be found in the Imperial State Crown. Both of these gems are kept on permanent display amongst the Crown Jewels in the Tower of London.

The blow which seemed to ruin the superb stone, in fact proved to be its making.

Sweet are the uses of adversity;
Which like the toad, ugly and venomous,
Wears yet a precious jewel in his head:
And this our life, exempt from public haunts
Finds tongues in trees, books in the running brooks
Sermons in stones, and good in everything.
(*As You Like It – William Shakespeare 1564–1616*)

READING:

St Ignatius Loyola (1491–1556): Born of a noble family, he embarked on a military career. In 1521 whilst fighting in the siege of Pampeluna he sustained a wound in the right leg. During his convalescence whilst reading the Life of Christ he decided to become a soldier of Christ.

The conversion of St Paul as described in his own words.
Acts 26, 4–23. 'My life from my youth up, the life I led from the beginning among my people and in Jerusalem, is familiar to all Jews. Indeed they have known me long enough and could testify, if they only would, that I belonged to the strictest group in our religion: I lived as a Pharisee. And it is for a hope kindled by God's promise to our forefathers that I stand in the dock today. Our twelve tribes hope to see the fulfilment of that promise, worshipping with intense devotion day and night; and for this very hope I am impeached, and impeached by Jews, Your Majesty. Why is it considered incredible among you that God should raise dead men to life?

I myself once thought it my duty to work actively against the name of Jesus of Nazareth; and I did so in Jerusalem. It was I who imprisoned many of God's people by authority obtained from the chief priests; and when they were condemned to death, my vote was cast against them. In all the synagogues I tried by repeated punishment to make them renounce their faith; indeed my fury rose to such a pitch that I extended my persecution to foreign cities.

On one such occasion I was travelling to Damascus with authority and commission from the chief priests; and as I was on my way, Your Majesty, in the middle of the day I saw a light from the sky, more brilliant than the sun, shining all around me and my travelling-companions. We all fell to the ground, and then I heard a voice saying to me in the Jewish language, 'Saul, Saul, why do you persecute me? It is hard for you, this kicking against the goad.' I said, 'Tell me, Lord, who are you'; and the Lord replied, 'I am Jesus, whom you are persecuting. But now, rise to your feet and stand upright. I have appeared to you for a purpose: to appoint you my servant and witness, to testify both to what you have seen and to what you shall yet see of me. I will rescue you from this people and from the Gentiles to whom I am sending you. I send you to open their eyes and turn them from darkness to light, from the dominion of Satan to God, so that, by trust in me, they may obtain forgiveness of sins, and a place with those whom God has made his own.'

And so, King Agrippa, I did not disobey the heavenly vision. I turned first to the inhabitants of Damascus, and then to Jerusalem and all the country of Judaea, and to the Gentiles, and sounded the call to repent and turn to God, and to prove their repentance by deeds. That is why the Jews seized me in the temple and tried to do away with me. But I had God's help, and so to this very day I stand and testify to great and small alike. I assert nothing beyond what was foretold by the prophets and by Moses: that the Messiah must suffer, and that he, the first to rise from the dead, would announce the dawn to Israel and to the Gentiles.'

PRAYER:

Teach us, good Lord,
To serve thee as thou deservest;
To give and not to count the cost;
To fight and not to heed the wounds;
To toil and not to seek for rest;
To labour and not to ask for any reward,
Save that of knowing that we do thy will.

(*Ignatius Loyola*)

Lord, when I am hungry, give me someone to feed,
When I am thirsty, give water for their thirst;
When I am sad, someone to lift from sorrow.
When burdens weigh upon me,
Lay upon my shoulders the burdens of my fellows.
Lord, when I stand greatly in need of tenderness
Give me someone who yearns for love.
May your will be my bread, your grace my strength,
Your love my resting place.

(*Translation from a French prayer, Anon*)

HYMNS: *Father, hear the prayer we offer*
Soldiers of Christ, arise

3

ACTIONS SPEAK LOUDER THAN WORDS

Aim: When God wished to demonstrate what a citizen of his Kingdom should be he became one of us and lived amongst us. Actions speak louder than words. God in Christ lived according to his own laws. He declared that it was not enough to talk about the truth, you have to live it. One of the greatest things about God is that he never demanded from any man what he was not prepared to do and give himself.

'God was in Christ reconciling the world to himself.'

(*2 Corinthians 5,19*)

'So the Word became flesh; he came to dwell among us, and we saw his glory, such glory as befits the Father's only Son, full of grace and truth.'

(*St John 1,14*)

Illustration:
There was an exceedingly clever cat and the mice were so plagued by her at every turn that they called a court to advise upon some way to prevent their being surprised. One member of the court said, 'If you will take my advice, there is nothing like hanging a bell round the cat's neck to give warning beforehand when she's coming.' They all regarded the suggestion as quite the best solution to their problem.

'Well,' said another, 'now that we are agreed upon the bell, who will put it round the cat's neck?' But there was no one who would agree to do that, and so the whole plan came to nothing.

'The boldest talkers are not always the greatest doers'.

(*Aesop*)

READING:

Philippians 2,5–11. 'Let your bearing towards one another arise out of your life in Christ Jesus. For the divine nature was his from the first; yet he did not think to snatch at equality with God, but made himself nothing, assuming the nature of a slave. Bearing the human likeness, revealed in human shape, he humbled himself, and in obedience accepted even death – death on a cross. Therefore God raised him to the heights and bestowed on him the name above all names, that at the name of Jesus every knee should bow – in heaven, on earth, and in the depths – and every tongue confess, "Jesus Christ is Lord", to the glory of God the Father.'

PRAYER:

Lord Jesus, help us,
To see more clearly the way we ought to take;
To know more fully the truth we ought to know;
To live more faithfully the life we ought to live.

Help us never to be satisfied
With words without deeds;
With plans without performance;
With schemes without results;
With dreams without toil to make the dream come true.
Teach us
That the way to the stars is always steep;
That sweat is the price of all things precious,
That there never can be any crown without a cross.
So make us willingly to spend life that we may gain life, and to take up our cross and follow in the footsteps of our Lord and Master, Jesus Christ. *Amen*.

(*William Barclay*)

HYMNS: *The people that in darkness sat*
Stand up, stand up for Jesus

4

IMPETUOSITY

Aim: Things aren't always what they appear to be.

'To know all is to forgive all'.

Illustration:
A young woman post office employee called into her favourite morning tea establishment and, with her tea and snack, bought a Moro* bar for afternoon sustenance. Why not, she thought during morning tea, buy another bar to eat tonight. So she went back to the counter and did just that.

Returning to her table she found a chap sitting there with a cup of coffee, a plate of cakes and munching wholeheartedly on her first Moro bar. She was, you will understand, quite beside herself. Speechless with rage, she snatched one of his cakes, took a whacking great

* A 'Moro' bar is a chocolate bar similar in taste to a Mars bar.

bite out of it, slammed it back down on his plate, picked up her handbag and stormed out. He, to say the least, looked astonished. Back at the office she opened her handbag and found her first Moro bar just where she had put it.

(*New Zealand Times*)

READINGS:

Judges 6,33–7,25. 'The Israelites were under siege, their land had been invaded by the combined armies of the Midianites, the Amalekites and the eastern desert tribes. The invading army was camped in the Vale of Jezreel. God calls Gideon to oppose the invaders; this he does successfully with a mere three hundred men. If the invaders had only known . . . !

Ephesians 4,32 and 5,1 & 2. 'Be generous to one another, tender-hearted, forgiving one another as God in Christ forgave you.

In a word, as God's dear children, try to be like him, and live in love as Christ loved you, and gave himself up on your behalf as an offering and sacrifice whose fragrance is pleasing to God.'

PRAYER:

Almighty God, renew us day by day by thy Holy Spirit. Let all quick temper and anger be put away from us. May we be kind to one another, tenderhearted, forgiving one another, even as thou, O Father, hast forgiven us for the sake of thy Son, Our Saviour Jesus Christ. *Amen*.

Bestow on us, O Lord, a kind spirit, and a gentle, loving and patient heart. Give us kindly looks, pleasant speech and friendly behaviour in our daily life; that we may give offence to none, but as much as in us lies live in peace with all our fellows. *Amen*.

HYMNS: *I bind myself to God today*
Help us, O Lord, to learn

use of talents
3

5

TALENTS

Aim: 'The Christian is a competitor in a life-long struggle for an eternal prize.'

(*B. F. Westcott*)

To be effective Christians we must be positive in our approach to life. It is no good just being neutral and bland. We must bring the same expertise, the same ingenuity and the same effort into our Christianity as a successful business man does to his business.

Illustration:

In medieval times when powerful barons could be troublesome to the king, the Baron of Elmley was summoned to appear before his monarch.

'I am tired of your proud and wilful ways,' said the King, 'and I intend to confiscate your lands.'

The baron begged to be spared.

'I will do anything you ask,' he cried, 'if you will only give me another chance.'

So sincere did the baron sound, and in the presence of so many courtiers, that the king, much against his better judgement, decided to offer the baron a challenge.

'Very well,' he replied, 'I will give you one more chance on condition that you are able to answer three questions which I shall put to you. The first is: how much am I worth? The second is: what is it that starts life walking on four legs, then on two, and finally on three? The third is: what am I thinking?'

The baron begged for time.

'Very well,' smiled the king confidently, 'I will give you a week.'

The baron left the court and sought out his friends to see if they could help, but with no success. Four days later, he was riding gloomily around his estate, thinking that all was lost, when he met one of his villagers.

The villager, taking off his cap, addressed the baron,

'Good afternoon sir,' he said.

The baron nodded his head and grunted.

'Begging your pardon, sir, I would like to offer my help in answering those questions put to you by the king.'

'That is very kind of you,' replied the baron, 'but they are very difficult. So difficult that none of my friends has come up with any likely answers.

'I promise you,' replied the villager, 'that if you exchange robes with me, and let me go to the king in your place, I will give the king satisfactory answers, and save your lands from being confiscated. After all,' he continued, 'we are about the same age and build, and if I were to trim my beard a little, I'd look like your double.'

The baron after some thought agreed to the suggestion.

On the appointed day, the villager dressed as the baron appeared before the King.

'Well,' said the King leaning back confidently on his throne, 'are you ready to answer my questions?'

'I am, your majesty,' replied the villager.

'Very well!' said the King. 'What am I worth?'

'Your majesty,' replied the villager, 'Jesus was sold for thirty pieces of silver. You cannot be worth more.'

The King could not challenge that assessment, and so he put his second question, 'What is it that starts life walking on four legs, then on two, and finally on three?'

The peasant replied, 'Man. He starts life crawling on all fours. He then learns to walk on two. And in old age he walks with the aid of a stick.'

The King once again had to agree. So he put his third and most difficult question, 'What am I thinking?'

'Your majesty,' smiled the villager, 'you are thinking that you are conversing with the Baron of Elmley, but in fact you are not, I am but a humble villager who lives on his estate.'

The King who had a sense of humour, burst out laughing.

'Well done!' he shouted, slapping the arm of his throne, 'You have answered my questions splendidly, and I shall let the Baron of Elmley keep his lands.'

READINGS:

St Matthew 10,16. 'Look, I send you out like sheep among wolves; be wary as serpents, innocent as doves.'

St Matthew 25,14–29. 'It is like a man going abroad, who called his servants and put his capital in their hands; to one he gave five bags of gold, to another two, to another one, each according to his capacity. Then he left the country. The man who had the five bags went at once and employed them in business, and made a profit of five bags, and the man who had the two bags made two. But the man who had been given one bag of gold went off and dug a hole in the ground, and hid his master's money. A long time afterwards their master returned, and proceeded to settle accounts with them. The man who had been given the five bags of gold came and produced the five he had made: "Master," he said, "you left five bags with me; look, I have made five more." "Well done, my good and trusty servant!" said the master. "You have proved trustworthy in a small way; I will now put you in charge of something big. Come and share your master's delight." The man with the two bags then came and said, "Master, you left two bags with me; look, I have made two more." "Well done, my good and trusty servant!" said the master. "You have proved trustworthy in a small way; I will now put you in charge of something big. Come and share your master's delight." Then the man who had been given one bag came and said, "Master, I knew you to be a hard man: you reap where you have not sown, you gather where you have not scattered; so I was afraid, and I went and hid your gold in the ground. Here it is – you have what belongs to you." "You lazy rascal!" said the master. "You knew that I reap where I have not sown, and gather where I have not scattered? Then you ought to have put my money on deposit, and on my return I should have got it back with interest. Take the bag of gold from him, and give it to the one with the ten bags." For the man who has will always be given more, till he has enough and to spare; and the man who has not will forfeit even what he has.'

PRAYER:

O God, by whose providence the duties of man are variously ordered: Grant to us all such a spirit that we may labour heartily to do our work in our several stations. Teach us to put to good account whatever talents thou has lent us, that as good and faithful servants we may enter into the joy of our Lord, even thy Son our Saviour Jesus Christ. *Amen.*

HYMNS: *God be in my head*
O Jesus I have promised

6

GRACE

Aim: Grace has been defined as 'a certain motion of the soul, bestowed by God for the production of some good act'.

Illustration:
Brian Boobbyer, who won blues in Cricket and Rugby at Oxford and went on to play centre threequarter for England, loves to retell the following incidents from the life of Victor Trumper.

Victor Trumper played cricket for Australia at the beginning of this century and is regarded as being one of the greatest stroke players the game has ever produced. He toured England with the Australian side and delighted capacity crowds with his artistry and fluent scoring. One of his most distinguished innings was against Yorkshire when he pulverized the bowling with a string of fours and sixes. Eventually, the Yorkshire captain gave the ball to a young coal miner who had recently joined the Club and totally lacking in first class experience. The young man was understandably anxious and nervous to be blooded against such a formidable bat, and no one would have blamed him had he failed to find his length. In the event, Trumper treated each ball with profound respect and made no attempt to take advantage of the young man's inexperience. On the contrary, he played him in, and allowed him to gather his confidence.

When questioned afterwards, Trumper admitted that he didn't want to spoil 'that lad's chance of getting a living in an easier way than heaving coal.'

There was a similar case in a match against Lancashire, at Liverpool. In the Lancashire side was a young bowler who, at enormous cost, had come over from Australia to try his luck in English cricket. Trumper knew that he was having a hard time and would be fortunate to keep his place in the Lancashire team. When he came on to bowl, Trumper approached each ball with great caution, and was finally bowled for six. Nobody said it, but many believed that Trumper gave him his wicket to help him along the way.

'For when the One Great Scorer comes
To write against your name,
He marks – not that you won or lost –
But how you played the game.'

(*Grantland Rice 1880–1954*)
Alumnus Football

READING:

Philippians 2,1–4. 'If then our common life in Christ yields anything to stir the heart, any loving consolation, any sharing of the Spirit, any warmth of affection or compassion, fill up my cup of happiness by thinking and feeling alike, with the same love for one another, the same turn of mind, and a common care for unity. Rivalry and personal vanity should have no place among you, but you should humbly reckon others better than yourselves. You must look to each other's interest and not merely to your own.'

PRAYERS:

Heavenly Father, we thank you alike for work and play. Help us to play fairly: to be modest and generous when we win, and cheerful when we lose. Teach us to value the game for its own sake and not for the prize which may be won. *Amen*.

O Lord God, give us grace to set a good example to all amongst whom we live; to be just and true in all our dealings, to be strict and conscientious in the discharge of every duty, pure and temperate in all enjoyment, kind and charitable and courteous toward all men; that so the mind of Jesus Christ may be formed in us, and all men take knowledge of us that we are his disciples; through the same Jesus Christ our Lord.

(*Dean Vaughan 1816–97*)

HYMNS: *O thou who camest from above*
Come down, O love divine

4 Ask Sue re Moonlight.

7

COMPASSION

Aim: Compassion has been described as an emotion which moves a man to the very depths of his being. It is that emotion which enables us to step into another person's shoes. It is the feeling that moved a king to forgive a servant who could not repay a debt (*Matthew 18,23–35*), that made a father welcome home his prodigal son (*Luke 15,11–24*), that made a Samaritan go to the help of a wounded traveller (*Luke 10,30–35*).

'I shall pass through this world but once. Any good thing therefore that I can do, or any kindness that I can show to any human being, let me do it now. Let me not defer it or neglect it, for I shall not pass this way again.'

Illustration:
Late one afternoon the composer Beethoven visited a local cobbler, to have a pair of shoes repaired. As he stood in the dingy workshop, he heard someone attempting to play the piano in a back room. He stood there listening because the person was trying to play one of Beethoven's pieces – but not very successfully. Turning to the cobbler he said,

'Who is that playing the piano?'

'My young daughter,' came the reply, 'but as you can hear, she's not very good. She's blind, and can only play from memory. Sometimes, when I can scrape a few coins together I take her to a concert, but that doesn't happen very often, I am afraid. And I cannot afford to send her for music lessons. It is a great pity really, because her only real joy is music.'

Beethoven placed his shoes on the workbench and said to the cobbler,

'May I go in and play for your daughter? You see, I play the piano and love music as well.'

The cobbler was delighted with the offer and led Beethoven into the tiny back room. He explained to his daughter about the kind man's offer, and placed a chair alongside her.

Gently and patiently Beethoven rehearsed the piece she had been playing, going over each bar again and again, until she was able to play it through without difficulty. So engrossed had he become with his new pupil, he failed to notice that darkness had fallen, and that he was playing by the light of the moon filtering through the small window.

Reluctantly he stopped when he realized how late it was.

'I am afraid I must go,' he said, 'I have an important engagement this evening, but I promise you, I will return to give you further lessons.'

As he got up to go, the blind girl reached out to touch him and thank him.

'What is your name sir?' she asked.

'I am the man who composed the music we've been playing this afternoon,' replied Beethoven.

'Not Mr Beethoven!' she gasped. 'Not Mr Beethoven the famous composer!'

'Yes, I am afraid so,' he said very gently, 'and I feel very honoured to have been allowed to spend this time with you.'

Late that night, after retiring to bed, Beethoven thought about the little blind girl struggling to play the piano, under almost impossible conditions. He recalled the room in which the piano stood, and the moon shining through the window illuminating the girl's hands as she sought for the correct keys. As these thoughts occupied his mind, he became so flooded with emotion that he could not fall asleep. Eventually, he got up and sat at his own piano and let his feelings flow. That night Beethoven composed one of the greatest pieces of music ever written, namely the *Moonlight Sonata*.

(If at all possible, this piece should be played.)

READINGS:

St Matthew 18,23–35.

St Luke 15,11–24.

St Luke 10,30–35. '"And who is my neighbour?" Jesus replied, "A man was on his way from Jerusalem down to Jericho when he fell in with robbers, who stripped him, beat him, and went off leaving him half dead. It so happened that a priest was going down by the same road; but when he saw him, he went past on the other side. So too a Levite came to the place, and when he saw him went past on the other side. But a Samaritan who was making the journey came upon him, and when he saw him was moved to pity. He went up and bandaged his wounds, bathing them with oil and wine. Then he lifted him on to his own beast, brought him to an inn, and looked after him there. Next day he produced two silver pieces and gave them to the innkeeper, and said, Look after him; and if you spend any more, I will repay you on my way back."'

PRAYER:

Christ has
  no body now on earth but yours;
  no hands but yours,
  no feet but yours.

Yours are the eyes
  through which is to look out
  Christ's compassion to the world.
Yours are the feet
  with which he is to go about
  doing good.
Yours are the hands
  with which he is to bless us now. *Amen*.

(*St Teresa of Avila*)

HYMNS: *Take my life and let it be*
Lord of all hopefulness, Lord of all joy

8

LOVE (I)

Aim: When the evening of this life comes, we shall be judged on love.
(*St John of the Cross*)

Illustration:
Love all God's creation, both the whole and every grain of sand. Love every leaf, every ray of light. Love the animals, love the plants, love each separate thing. If thou love each thing then thou wilt perceive the mystery of God in all; and when thou perceivest this, then thou wilt thenceforward grow every day to a fuller understanding of it.
(*F. Dostoevsky, The Brothers Karamazov*)

In Africa, when they have a specially heavy burden to carry, they tie it to one end of a stick, then they tie a stone of equal weight to the other end of the stick, and then they carry the stick and the two burdens across their shoulders. The one balances the other, and two burdens are easier than one. Start carrying someone else's load, and you can forget your own.

(*William Barclay, In the Hands of God*)

READING:
1 Corinthians 13. Though I speak with the tongues of men and of angels, and have not love, I am become as sounding brass,

or a tinkling cymbal. And though I have the gift of prophecy, and understand all mysteries, and all knowledge; and though I have all faith, so that I could remove mountains, and have no love, I am nothing. And though I bestow all my goods to feed the poor, and though I give my body to be burned, and have not love, it profiteth me nothing.

Love suffereth long and is kind; love envieth not; love vaunteth not itself, is not puffed up, doth not behave itself unseemly, seeketh not her own, is not easily provoked, thinketh no evil; rejoiceth not in iniquity, but rejoiceth in the truth; beareth all things, believeth all things, hopeth all things, endureth all things. Love never faileth: but whether there be prophecies, they shall fail; whether there be tongues, they shall cease; whether there be knowledge, it shall vanish away. For we know in part, and we prophesy in part. But when that which is perfect is come, then that which is in part shall be done away. When I was a child, I spake as a child, I understood as a child, I thought as a child: but when I became a man, I put away childish things. For now we see through a glass, darkly; but then face to face: now I know in part; but then shall I know even as also I am known. And now abideth faith, hope, love, these three; but the greatest of these is love.'

PRAYER:

Lord, make us instruments of thy peace.
Where there is hatred, let us sow love;
Where there is injury, pardon;
Where there is discord, union;
Where there is doubt, faith;
Where there is despair, hope;
Where there is darkness, light;
Where there is sadness, joy;

O Divine Master, grant that we may
not so much seek to be consoled as to console;
to be understood as to understand;
to be loved as to love;
through the love of thy Son who died for us,
Jesus Christ our Lord. *Amen.*

(*St Francis of Assisi*)

HYMNS: *Gracious Spirit, Holy Ghost*
Give me joy in my heart

9

LOVE (II)

Aim: True religion is to love, as God has loved, all things both great and small.

(*Hindu*)

Illustration – God Is Love

Though I speak the most cultured English and have great powers of oratory and conversation, but in my heart have not the language of love and sympathy, I am become as blatant as a noisy horn or as empty as a tinkling brass bell.

And though I am well versed in all world problems, and read volumes of books and am considered by my friends as well educated, and though I am an optimist and believe that everything will come out all right in the end, but have not love in my heart to see the suffering of people oppressed by those world problems, my knowledge is a vacant thing.

And though I contribute to all the city charities, and deny myself of many luxuries, and even deny my body of the necessities of life, and yet do it with a sense of self-pride and not for love of my fellowman, my charity is as cold as the word itself.

Love makes me suffer with all who suffer; love makes me kind; love takes envy of others good fortune from my heart so that I can rejoice with them, and then when my own good fortune comes, love keeps me from flaunting my wealth before the less fortunate.

For love will not let me behave boastfully, nor graspingly, nor will it let me be impatient with others' shortcomings, nor will it let me listen to the evil gossip of others. But rather, love lets me see the beauty and the good qualities of my fellowmen. It shows me how I can help to share their burdens; it gives me hope that the sorrows of the world can be lifted by the undergirding arms of enduring love.

For true love has never failed. Man's prophecies for the future world will fail. Man's great flights of oratory will be forgotten. His best-selling books will crumble into dust. For no man has all knowledge nor can he see all of the future. But love is all-powerful and all-perfect, and if we will let it control our lives, then our future is as secure as the love of Christ.

When I was a child, my speech, my thoughts, my understanding were that of a child; but now I am an adult, and I must assume an adult's responsibility in the world.

But not until love has become the complete rule of my life – not until my actions, my judgments of other people – my entire life is based on the principle of love, will I achieve the glory which can come to a true follower of the Christ, whose life was Love.

And now abideth faith, hope, love, these three, but the greatest of these is love.

(*Hilda E. Koontz, World Christian Digest, Autumn 1948*)

READING:

1 Corinthians 13.

PRAYER:

O Lord Jesus Christ,
Take our hands, and work with them;
Take our lips, and speak through them;
Take our minds, and think with them;
Take our hearts, and set them on fire
With love for thee and for all mankind
For Thy sake. *Amen.*

(*Warwick School*)

HYMNS: *Love divine, all loves excelling*
Help us to help each other Lord

10

LOVE (III)

Aim: Love is as strong as death
Many waters cannot quench love.

(*Song of Songs, 8,6 & 7*)

Illustration:

(*An Indian paraphrase of I Cor. 13*)

If I have the language ever so perfectly and speak like a Pundit, and have not the knack of love that grips the heart, I am nothing. If I have decorations and diplomas, and am proficient in up to date methods, and have not the touch of an understanding love, I am nothing.

If I am able to worst my opponents in argument so as to make fools of them, and have not the wooing note, I am nothing.

If I have all faith and great ideas and magnificent plans, and wonderful vision, and have not the love that sweats and bleeds and weeps and prays and pleads, I am nothing.

If I give no end of money to benefit the poor and have not the love to take them into my home sometimes, I am nothing.

If I surrender all prospects, and leaving home and friends and comforts, give myself to the self-evident sacrifice of the missionary career and turn sour and selfish amid the daily annoyances and personal slights of a missionary's life, and though I give my body to be consumed in the heat and sweat and mildew of India, and have not the love that yields its rights, its coveted leisure, its pet plans, I am nothing – nothing. Virtue has ceased to go out from me.

If I can heal all manner of sicknesses and disease, but wound hearts and hurt feelings for want of love that is kind, I am nothing.

If I can write books and publish articles that set the world agog, and fail to transcribe the word of the Cross into the language of love, I am nothing; worse, if I have not this love, I may be competent, busy, fussy, punctilious, well-equipped, but, like the Church at Laodicea, nauseating to Christ.

(*Practical Christianity, World Christian Digest, November 1950*)

READING:

Colossians 3,12–17. 'Then put on the garments that suit God's chosen people, his own, his beloved: compassion, kindness, humility, gentleness, patience. Be forbearing with one another, and forgiving, where any of you has cause for complaint: you must forgive as the Lord forgave you. To crown all, there must be love, to bind all together and complete the whole. Let Christ's peace be arbiter in your hearts: to this peace you were called as members of a single body. And be filled with gratitude. Let the message of Christ dwell among you in all its richness. Instruct and admonish each other with the utmost wisdom. Sing thankfully in your hearts to God, with psalms and hymns and spiritual songs. Whatever you are doing, whether you speak or act, do everything in the name of the Lord Jesus, giving thanks to God the Father through him.'

PRAYER:

O Lord who hast taught us that all our doings without love are nothing worth: send thy Holy Spirit and pour into our hearts that most excellent gift of love, the very bond of peace and of all virtues, without which whosoever liveth is counted dead before thee: grant this for thine only Son Jesus Christ's sake. *Amen*.

(*Archbishop Cranmer*)

HYMNS: *Breathe on me, Breath of God*
O Holy Spirit, Lord of grace

11

LOVE (IV)

Aim: God himself dwells in us if we love one another.

(*1 John 4.8*)

Illustration:

I Corinthians 13

I may have a gift of oratory surpassing Winston Churchill
But if I have no love
I have become like the senseless din of a screaming jet
the howl of a racing-car exhaust
or the jangling of a go-go girl.
I may have the gift of inspired preaching and be another Billy Graham
Or see my way through the mysteries of the Kingdom of God
as a New Theologian
a Liturgical reformer
or an Ecumenical enthusiast.
I may have all knowledge that man can attain, and be
a transplanter of hearts
a penetrator of space
a conqueror of cancer.

Or, on the other hand, I may have all the fullness of faith
so that my orthodoxy towers over the petty heresies of the moment
so that the intensity of my faith could move mountains.
Yet – if I have no love
so far from being a Christian of some account
I am a feeble fake.
I may be a beacon light of generosity
a leader in the planned-giving campaign in my parish
a philanthropist who has endowed a trust
one who has already made his will which includes a large gift to the church.
I may even be a martyr like Lawrence on his grill
or Ridley at the stake
or a Buddhist monk on a Vietnamese footpath
But – if I have no love
so far from being a saint or hero
or receiving any reward in heaven
I am a foolish fraud.
Love is the one thing that counts –
Love is patient and kind
Love has no hatred or envy
It is never boastful and brash – or swollen with self-importance
It never oversteps what is seemly – or demands its pound of flesh
It never roars with rage
It keeps no museum of stored resentments,
It finds no secret pleasure in the human failings of others
but joyously responds to truth, honesty and goodness.
It is tolerant to a fault.
A Christian does not allow himself to be fooled by every rogue
but where there is a doubt
he gives the benefit of it.
Love is the trigger of a hope that never dies
Love is no weak, simpering, sentimental thing
It is the ultimate in strength
There will never be a time when love dies.
There will be a day when all the hypotheses of scholarship will have lost enchantment . . . even for the scholars
There will be an hour when all the flashy accoutrements of religion will lie worm-ridden amongst the garbage
There will be a moment when it will not matter twopence what school you went to or what sort of degree you obtained.
For all our knowledge and all our preaching are but fragments of the whole

And when the absolute completeness of eternity is achieved
Then these little fragments of understanding to what we cling
will be as insignificant as rock pools
in our comprehension of the ocean.
Love is the key to the eternal
for when absolute completeness shall come
then our fragmentary knowledge will bė of little use.
The difference between NOW and THEN is far greater
than that which distinguishes a child from a man –
yet even here the change is clear.
When I was a child, my words were childish
my thoughts were childish
my reason was childish
but when I became a man – this has all changed.
Or, change the illustration,
Our present understanding is like the reflection
of a friend's face in a cheap mirror
It is distorted and shadowy, twisted and unreal
But in eternity, our understanding is clear –
it is like meeting our friend face to face.
Our present knowledge and wisdom is like half a dozen pieces of a jigsaw puzzle,
But in Eternity
we have all the pieces
the picture is clear
And I shall know as completely as God has known me from the beginning.
So then, living in TIME as we do, worldly knowledge seems important
But when we move into ETERNITY, we slough off our knowledge as a chrysalis
and three things only remain constant
the three things we take with us on this journey –
They are Faith – Hope and Love.
And the greatest of these is Love.
To live is to love – there is no other life.

(*Ian Shevill, 'Going it – with God'*)

READING:

St Luke 10,25–37. 'On one occasion a lawyer came forward to put this test question to him: "Master, what must I do to inherit eternal life?" Jesus said, "What is written in the Law? What is your reading of it?" He replied, "Love the Lord your

God with all your heart, with all your soul, with all your strength, and with all your mind; and your neighbour as yourself." "That is the right answer," said Jesus; "do that and you will live."

But he wanted to vindicate himself, so he said to Jesus, "And who is my neighbour?" Jesus replied, "A man was on his way from Jerusalem down to Jericho when he fell in with robbers, who stripped him, beat him, and went off leaving him half dead. It so happened that a priest was going down by the same road; but when he saw him, he went past on the other side. So too a Levite came to the place, and when he saw him went past on the other side. But a Samaritan who was making the journey came upon him, and when he saw him was moved to pity. He went up and bandaged his wounds, bathing them with oil and wine. Then he lifted him on to his own beast, brought him to an inn, and looked after him there. Next day he produced two silver pieces and gave them to the Innkeeper, and said, Look after him; and if you spend any more, I will repay you on my way back. Which of these three do you think was neighbour to the man who fell into the hands of the robbers?" He answered, "The one who showed him kindness." Jesus said, "Go and do as he did."'

PRAYERS:

Grant that we may walk as Christ walked; grant that what the Spirit was in him, such he may be also in us; grant that our lives may be refashioned after the pattern of his life; grant that we may do today here on earth what Christ would have done, and in the way he would have done it; grant that we may become vessels of his grace, instruments of his will, to thy glory and honour: through Jesus Christ our Lord. *Amen.*

(*J. H. Jowett*)

To God the Father, who first loved us, and made us
accepted in the Beloved:
To God the Son, who loved us, and washed us from
our sins in his own blood:
To God the Holy Spirit, who sheds the love of God
abroad within our hearts:
Be all love and all glory
For time and for eternity. *Amen.*

HYMNS: *Come down, O Love divine*
Take my life, and let it be

12

LOVE (V)

Aim: Hatred is never diminished by hatred. Hatred is diminished by love. This is the eternal law.

(*Buddhist*)

Illustration:
In '41 Mama took me back to Moscow. There I saw our enemies for the first time. If my memory is right, nearly twenty thousand German war prisoners were to be marched in a single column through the streets of Moscow.

The pavements swarmed with onlookers, cordoned off by soldiers and police.

The crowd were mostly women – Russian women with hands roughened by hard work, lips untouched by lipstick, and thin hunched shoulders which had borne half the burden of the war. Every one of them must have had a father or a husband, a brother or a son killed by the Germans.

They gazed with hatred in the direction from which the column was to appear.

At last we saw it.

The generals marched at the head, massive chins stuck out, lips folded disdainfully, their whole demeanor meant to show superiority over their plebeian victors.

The women were clenching their fists. The soldiers and policemen had all they could do to hold them back.

All at once something happened to them.

They saw German soldiers, thin, unshaven, wearing dirty blood-stained bandages, hobbling on crutches or leaning on the shoulders of their comrades; the soldiers walked with their heads down.

The street became dead silent – the only sound was the shuffling of boots and the thumping of crutches.

Then I saw an elderly woman in broken-down boots push herself forward and touch a policeman's shoulder, saying: 'Let me through.' There must have been something about her that made him step aside.

She went up to the column, took from inside her coat something wrapped in a coloured handkerchief and unfolded it. It was a crust of black bread. She pushed it awkwardly into the pocket of a soldier, so exhausted that he was tottering on his feet. And now suddenly from every side women were running towards the soldiers, pushing into their hands bread, cigarettes, whatever they had.

The soldiers were no longer enemies.

They were people.

(*Yevgeny Yevtushenko, A Precocious Autobiography, Penguin Books*)

READING:

1 John 4,7–21. 'Dear friends, let us love one another, because love is from God. Everyone who loves is a child of God and knows God, but the unloving know nothing of God. For God is love; and his love was disclosed to us in this, that he sent his only Son into the world to bring us life. The love I speak of is not our love for God, but the love he showed to us in sending his Son as the remedy for the defilement of our sins. If God thus loved us, dear friends, we in turn are bound to love one another. Though God has never been seen by any man, God himself dwells in us if we love one another; his love is brought to perfection within us.

Here is the proof that we dwell in him and he dwells in us; he has imparted his Spirit to us. Moreover, we have seen for ourselves, and we attest, that the Father sent the Son to be the saviour of the world, and if a man acknowledges that Jesus is the Son of God, God dwells in him and he dwells in God. Thus we have come to know and believe the love which God has for us.

God is love; he who dwells in love is dwelling in God, and God in him. This is for us the perfection of love, to have confidence on the day of judgement, and this we can have, because even in this world we are as he is. There is no room for fear in love; perfect love banishes fear. For fear brings with it the pains of judgement, and anyone who is afraid has not attained to love in its perfection. We love because he loved us first. But if a man says, "I love God", while hating his brother, he is a liar. If he does not love the brother whom he has seen, it cannot be that he loves God whom he has not seen. And indeed this command comes to us from Christ himself: that he who loves God must also love his brother.'

PRAYER:

Lord, when I am hungry, give me someone to feed,
When I am thirsty, give water for their thirst;
When I am sad, someone to lift from sorrow.

When burdens weigh upon me,
Lay upon my shoulders the burdens of my fellows.
Lord, when I stand greatly in need of tenderness
Give me someone who yearns for love.
May your will be my bread, your grace my strength,
Your love my resting place. *Amen.*

(*Translation from a French prayer. ANON*)

HYMNS: *Thy kingdom come, O God*
O day of God, draw nigh

13

KINDNESS

Aim: I expect to pass through this world but once. Any good thing, therefore, that I can do, or any kindness that I can show to any fellow creature, let me do it now. Let me not defer or neglect it, for I shall not pass this way again.

(*Anon*)

Illustration:
In any town or city we are very likely to come across someone playing a musical instrument on a street corner or open space in the hope that passers-by will throw a coin or two in their direction. We call these musicians buskers, and they have been around for centuries.

On one occasion the world famous violinist Paganini happened to be walking along a street in Paris, when he came across a poor old man standing in the gutter scraping out a miserable tune on a cheap violin. He was trying to earn a few coppers. But none of the passers-by took any notice of him. Indeed, if anything, they quickened their step to get out of earshot. Paganini slipped his hand into his pocket for a coin, only to discover that he had come without any money. He paused, and then, stepping into the gutter alongside the old man, he smiled and gently took the violin and bow from the old man's hands, and began to play. The music that flowed from the violin was exquisite. People began to stop and listen. Soon a large crowd gathered. Someone recognized who the player was, and soon the whisper spread, 'It's Paganini. It's Paganini!'

After some ten minutes, Paganini told the old man to pass his hat round the crowd. He did so and met with so generous a response – that his hat was filled to the brim. Paganini continued to play a little while longer to the delight of his audience and then, handing back the violin and bow to the old man, he continued on his way.

READING:

1 John 4,20 & 21. 'We love because he loved us first. But if a man says, "I love God", while hating his brother, he is a liar. If he does not love the brother whom he has seen, it cannot be that he loves God whom he has not seen. And indeed this command comes to us from Christ himself: that he who loves God must also love his brother.'

PRAYER:

Christ has
  no body now on earth but yours;
  no hands but yours;
  no feet but yours;
Yours are the eyes
  through which is to look out
  Christ's compassion to the world.
Yours are the feet
  with which he is to go about
  doing good.
Yours are the hands
  with which he is to bless us now. *Amen.*

HYMNS: *When I needed a neighbour*
Jesus, Lord, we look to thee

14

PROVIDENCE

Aim: There is a divinity that shapes our ends,
Rough-hew them how we will.

(*William Shakespeare, Hamlet*)

Let him who seeks cease not from seeking until he find; and when he finds he shall be astonished; astonished, he shall gain the Kingdom; and having gained the Kingdom, he shall have rest.

(*The Gospel of Thomas*)

The reason why the element of paradox comes into all religious thought and statement is because God cannot be comprehended in any human words or in any categories of our finite thought.

(*D. M. Baillie, God was in Christ*)

Illustration:
One of the most distinguished and honoured of American bishops during the nineteenth century was Bishop Wippell of Minnesota. In 1898 the bishop visited London for the Lambeth Conference. During the Conference a fellow bishop approached him and asked him to do him a special favour.

'I have a friend,' he said, 'who has been the Vicar of a slum parish in New York for the past thirty years. He wrote to me recently telling me how discouraged and depressed he felt. I wonder whether you would be kind enough to call on him on your way home, to cheer him up a little?'

Bishop Wippell immediately agreed to do this; and his fellow bishop wrote the Vicar's name and address on a piece of paper. When Bishop Wippell saw the name, he said,

'I have heard of this man and I shall look forward to meeting him.'

When Bishop Wippell arrived in New York, he called on the Vicar, who welcomed him into his home. Gently the Bishop encouraged the Vicar to share his thoughts with him.

'I have served God in this parish for the last thirty years,' said the Vicar. 'I have put my heart and soul into my work. I have visited my flock diligently; I have nurtured the sick; I have looked after the youth; I have said my prayers; I have always thoroughly prepared my sermons; I have conducted the Church services as beautifully as I can.

Yet, in spite of all this, I cannot see any sign of progress. In fact, if I am to be honest, the church is not as flourishing as it was when I first arrived. I feel a complete failure.'

The Bishop gently took the old man's hand in his and said,

'Do you remember preparing a young woman called Emma Smith for Confirmation, some twenty five years ago?'

The Vicar thought for a while and then replied,

'Yes, I vaguely recall her. I believe she headed out West. I haven't heard about her since.'

'You are quite right,' replied the Bishop, 'she went out West and got a job as a housekeeper on a remote farm. She looked after the farmer and his three grown up sons. The farmer's wife had died some years previously, and father and sons had become brutalized and coarse through isolation, hard work and heavy drinking. After Emma had been at the farm for a couple of years, the eldest son said to her one day, 'I do not know how you can stick it here with a lot like us!'

The woman replied, 'I could not if it were not for my religion.'

'Tell me about it,' said the eldest son.

'I cannot tell you much,' she replied, 'because I am not educated. But you can read the notes which I made during my Confirmation lessons.' This the eldest son did and then got in touch with a clergyman who lived about thirty miles away and obtained further instruction. Later, he took his share of the family property, went to College, offered himself for ordination and was accepted. And that eldest son is now the Bishop of Minnesota, who is sitting talking to you at this moment. So you see, my friend, your labours have not been wasted. Had it not been for you, I would most certainly never have become a bishop.'

(*As told by The Revd Lewis Davies*)

READING:

Romans 8,29–39. 'For God knew his own before ever they were, and also ordained that they should be shaped to the likeness of his Son, that he might be the eldest among a large family of brothers; and it is these, so fore-ordained, whom he has also called. And those whom he called he has justified, and to those whom he justified he has also given his splendour.

With all this in mind, what are we to say? If God is on our side, who is against us? He did not spare his own Son, but surrendered him for us all; and with this gift how can he fail to lavish upon us all he has to give? Who will be the accuser of God's chosen ones? It is God who pronounces acquittal: then who can condemn? It is Christ – Christ who died, and, more than that, was raised from the dead – who is at God's right hand, and indeed pleads our cause. Then what can separate us from the love of Christ? Can affliction or hardship? Can persecution, hunger, nakedness, peril, or the sword? "We are being done to death for thy sake all day long," as Scripture says; "we have been treated like sheep for slaughter" – and yet, in spite of all, overwhelming victory is ours through him who loved us. For I am convinced that there is nothing in death or life, in the realm of spirits or superhuman powers, in the world as it is or the world as it shall be, in the forces of the universe, in heights or depths – nothing in all creation that can separate us from the love of God in Christ Jesus our Lord.'

PRAYERS:

Teach us, good Lord
To serve thee as thou deservest;
To give and not to count the cost;
To fight and not to heed the wounds;
To toil and not to seek for rest;
To labour and not to ask for any reward,
Save that of knowing that we do thy will. *Amen.*

(*Ignatius Loyola*)

O Holy Spirit, giver of light and life,
Impart to us thoughts higher than our own thoughts
and prayers better than our own prayers,
and powers beyond our own powers,
that we may spend and be spent
in the ways of love and goodness,
after the perfect image
of our Lord and Saviour Jesus Christ. *Amen.*

(*Daily Prayer*)

HYMNS: *God moves in a mysterious way*
Be thou my vision, O Lord of my heart

15

OBEDIENCE

Aim: Society cannot function without laws and agreed codes of behaviour, e.g. What would happen if we ignored red traffic lights? What would happen in a school if we ignored the timetable? How could we play games without laws? However, from time to time laws need amending, and there is a correct way of setting about this. To act unilaterally is to create chaos.

St Francis was a very simple man, but through him flowed divine wisdom. The following story may sound absurd but yet . . .

Illustration:
St Francis of Assisi was one of the most remarkable men of the Middle Ages. He was the son of a wealthy merchant. When he was a young man, he lived a life of pleasure and luxury; but one day he felt called to give that all up and devote his life to simplicity of living, to prayer and good works. He renounced all his wealth, left his parents home and started on a life of complete poverty, wandering round the country, preaching about Christ, begging for his food, sleeping in caves or any shelter he could find. His devotion to a life of poverty and prayer was so great that people began to follow him and accept him as their leader, and he became the founder of the Franciscan Order of Friars. His influence has been world-wide and lasting.

At one time he and a few of his followers lived in a cave at Monte Casala north of Perugia in Italy. One day two young men came to him saying that they wanted to become his followers. Francis looked at the young men and said,

'Before accepting you, I would like you to do something for me.'

As he said this, he stooped down, picked up two cabbage plants, and handed one to each of the young men. Pointing to a small patch of newly dug soil, he asked them to plant the cabbages. As they made to go, Francis added, 'There is just one thing more, I would like you to plant them upside-down, so that the leaves are buried and the roots are in the air.'

One of the young men picked up a trowel, and planted the cabbage as directed by Francis. The other young man paused, and after considering the request, said, 'That is not the way to plant cabbages! They would never grow like that!'

Francis smiled at him and said, 'I agree with you, but that was not the object of the exercise. I think that you had better return home. There is no room in the Order for you.'

Turning to the other young man, Francis extended his hand and said, 'I bid you welcome into the Order, I am sure that you will be a valued member.'

Today, if you go to Monte Casala, you will find a little monastery built into the side of a wooded mountain, overlooking the most spectacular and breath-taking scenery. Inside the walled garden you will find the same cabbage patch, carefully tended, with just a few cabbages growing – the right way up of course!

(*Dr Richard Frost*)

READINGS:

St Mark 6,7–10. 'On one of his teaching journeys round the villages he summoned the Twelve and sent them out in pairs on a mission. He gave them authority over unclean spirits, and instructed them to take nothing for the journey beyond a stick: no bread, no pack, no money in their belts. They might wear sandals, but not a second coat. "When you are admitted to a house", he added, "stay there until you leave those parts. At any place where they will not receive you or listen to you, shake the dust off your feet as you leave, as a warning to them."'

St Mark 10,17–22. '"Good Master, what must I do to win eternal life?" Jesus said to him, "Why do you call me good? No one is good except God alone. You know the commandments: Do not murder; do not commit adultery; do not steal; do not give false evidence; do not defraud; honour your father and mother." "But, Master," he replied, "I have kept all these since I was a boy." Jesus looked straight at him; his heart warmed to him, and he said, "One thing you lack: go, sell everything you have, and give to the poor, and you will have riches in heaven; and come, follow me." At these words his face fell and he went away with a heavy heart; for he was a man of great wealth."

Romans 13,1–6. 'Every person must submit to the supreme authorities. There is no authority but by act of God, and the existing authorities are instituted by him; consequently anyone who rebels against authority is resisting a divine institution, and those who so resist have themselves to thank for the punishment they will receive. For government, a terror to crime, has no terrors for good behaviour. You wish to have no fear of the authorities? Then continue to do right and you will have their approval, for they are God's agents working for your good. But if you are doing wrong, then you will have cause to fear them; it is not for nothing that they hold the power of the sword, for they are God's agents of punishment, for retribution on the offender. That is why you are obliged to submit. It is an obligation imposed not merely by fear of retribution but by conscience. That is also why you pay taxes. The authorities are in God's service and to these duties they devote their energies.'

PRAYERS:

Speak, Lord, for thy servant heareth.
Grant us ears to hear
Eyes to see,
Wills to obey,
Hearts to love;
Then declare what thou wilt,
Reveal what thou wilt,
Command what thou wilt,
Demand what thou wilt.

(*Christina Rossetti 1830–1894*)

O Lord, renew our spirits and draw our hearts unto thyself, that our work may not be to us a burden, but a delight; and give us such a mighty love to thee as may sweeten all our obedience.
O, let us not serve thee with the spirit of bondage as slaves, but with cheerfulness and gladness of children, delighting ourselves in thee and rejoicing in thy work. *Amen.*

(*Benjamin Jenks*)

HYMNS: *When I survey the wondrous Cross*
Take my life, and let it be

16

LIGHT

Aim: Unless we share our Christianity, unless we give it to others, we lose it.

'By gaining his life a man will lose it; by losing his life for my sake, he will gain it.'

(*St Matthew 10,39*)

Illustration:
Thirteen centuries ago there was a priest called Rhidian who looked after a small church in what is now known as the Gower peninsula. Rhidian decided to make the long pilgrimage to the shrine of St David situated on the remote coastline of Dyfed in West Wales. The journey was difficult and arduous because there were no roads in those days only rough tracks, and rivers either had to be waded or crossed by ferry. Eventually, he arrived at David's burial place and made his offering. Before returning, he lit a small lamp he had brought with him, from the flame which burnt on the altar of the shrine. It was his great wish to light the lamp in his own church from the sacred flame. All the way home he carefully guarded the flame, shielding it from winds and drafts and constantly checking on the oil level.

As he neared his journey's end, he stayed over night with a neighbouring priest of his called Gwynor. They shared a simple meal and then said their evening prayers before retiring to bed. Gwynor could not help noticing how attentive Rhidian was to his lamp. Eventually Gwynor said to Rhidian, 'Why do you keep glancing at your lamp? Indeed, why do you keep your lamp alight when mine is sufficient to illuminate the room?'

'Ah!' said Rhidian. 'This flame is sacred, it comes from the flame which burns on the altar of the shrine of David our patron saint.'

'Really!' came the surprised reply. 'What are you going to do with it?'

'I am going to use it to light the lamp which hangs over the altar of my own church,' replied Rhidian.

There was a pause, and then Gwynor said, 'I don't suppose you would let me light the altar lamp of my church from your sacred flame? I think it is a lovely idea.'

Rhidian hesitated for a moment, his immediate reaction was to refuse, because after all it was his idea, and it was he who had made the pilgrimage and so carefully cherished the flame. But because he was a saintly man, he agreed to Gwynor's request.

The following morning he set out on the last lap of his journey, a matter of some ten miles or so. He had not gone very far when the most awful blizzard of snow and wind swept in from the sea. Rhidian did everything to protect and shield his lamp, but in vain, the wind was too powerful and the flame was blown out. He was desolate! As he stood there with the wind and snow swirling about him, he remembered that he had shared the flame with Gwynor. He immediately retraced his steps and rekindled his lamp. As he did so he recalled how near he had come to refusing to share the flame and said to himself, 'I would never have had my light unless I had given it away.'

READINGS:

St Matthew 5,14–16. 'You are light for all the world. A town that stands on a hill cannot be hidden. When a lamp is lit, it is not put under the meal-tub, but on the lamp-stand, where it gives light to everyone in the house. And you, like the lamp, must shed light among your fellows, so that, when they see the good you do, they may give praise to your Father in heaven.'

Ephesians 5,6–20.

PRAYERS:

O Holy Spirit, the Comforter, come and dwell in our souls; make our bodies thy temple. Fill our minds with thy light, and our hearts with thy love, that over our whole character thy power may be seen in the beauties of holiness. May we live as something sacred to thee as well as perfected by thee. Come in all thy sevenfold energy, and replenish us with thy illuminating, comforting, sanctifying influence. Baptize us with celestial fire, and give us in thine abundant grace the gift of everlasting life. *Amen.*

(*John Angell James, 1785–1859*)

Grant that we may walk as Christ walked; grant that what the Spirit was in him, such he may be also in us; grant that our lives may be refashioned after the pattern of his life; grant that we may do today here on earth what Christ would have done, and in the way he would have done it; grant that we may become vessels of his grace, instruments of his will, to thy honour and glory: through Jesus Christ our Lord. *Amen.*

(*J. H. Jowett*)

HYMNS: *Awake, awake: fling off the night!*
We have a gospel to proclaim

17

WITNESS

Aim: The word 'witness' comes from an old English word 'witan' which means 'someone who knows and is therefore able to tell'. The Church is made up of people who have been called apart by God to be witnesses of his, to proclaim the Gospel (Good News). A Christian has been called to be a light, to enlighten those who still live in darkness.

'The Lord is my light and my salvation'.

(*Psalm 27,1*)

Illustration:

There was once a king who had two grown-up sons, both of whom he loved dearly. In that land it did not follow that the first-born became heir to the throne. The king, therefore, could choose either one of his children to succeed him. So, to be scrupulously fair, he summoned both of his sons into his presence and said,

'I find the task of deciding which one of you will inherit the throne after me very difficult. I love you equally, and I think that you are both able and clever. Above all, I would hate you to think that I favoured one rather than the other. So I have decided to submit you to a test. Tomorrow at dawn, I shall give each of you a silver coin (worth about one pound). You will be given the whole day in which to purchase something which will fill the palace. The one who succeeds will inherit the throne. Do you accept my proposal as being fair?'

The two sons agreed that this was a fair and just way of deciding which of them would be the next king.

The following day at dawn, the brothers set out on their mission. The elder brother headed for a farm and asked the farmer how much straw could be obtained in exchange for his silver coin. The farmer showed him, and the elder brother realized that the amount wouldn't fill one of the smallest of the palace rooms. He continued his search all day, and then, when he was on the point of returning to the farmer and settling for a load of straw, he came across a shepherd playing on his pipes.

'Ah!' thought the elder brother, 'I have got it! What a marvellous idea!'

Approaching the shepherd he said,

'Would you sell me your pipes in exchange for this silver coin?'

The shepherd, without hesitation, agreed.

The elder brother immediately headed for home, clutching the pipes triumphantly in his hand.

Meanwhile the younger brother had set out for the market place in the nearby town. He visited all the stalls, but could find nothing which would fill his father's palace in exchange for one silver coin. He visited the mattress-maker and asked him how great a quantity of feathers he could buy for a silver coin. When the mattress-maker showed him, he realized that it would not be sufficient to fill even the smallest room in the servants' quarters. He continued his search and the hours slipped by remorselessly, and soon the evening shadows began to steal across the market square and people began to light their lamps. It was then that inspiration came! He rushed into the candlemaker's shop just as the door was being closed and asked,

'How many of your smallest candles can I purchase for this silver coin?'

The candlemaker showed him.

'I will buy them,' said the younger son, 'please wrap them up for me.' And so, placing the parcel firmly under his arm, he headed for the palace.

When he arrived, the king and his elder son were waiting, and when the elder son saw how small a parcel his brother was carrying, he smiled confidently to himself.

'Now then,' said the king, 'let us begin,' and turning to his elder son, he said, 'Show me what you have bought which will fill my palace.'

The elder brother produced his pipes and said,

'I shall fill your palace with music.' Whereupon he began to play, first quietly and then with increasing volume.

'There,' he said, 'I have filled the palace with music.'

'Well done my son,' said the king, most impressed, 'so you have! So you have!'

But the younger brother interrupted and said,

'I do not think that the sound of the pipes reached every part of the palace. I do not think, for example, it reached the cellars or the attics.'

'Hm,' muttered the king, 'we will have to find out.'

So servants were sent to the attics and cellars and asked to listen and report back. When they returned they all said that they had not heard any sound of music.

'Nevertheless,' said the king, 'a great part of the palace has been filled.' Turning to his younger son, he said, 'Can you improve on your brother's performance?'

The younger son opened his parcel, to reveal dozens of tiny candles. These he distributed amongst the servants and ordered them to place a candle in every room, hall, passage and cellar, and light them. This was done and the palace was filled with light.

READINGS:

Psalm 15

'O Lord, who may lodge in thy tabernacle?
Who may dwell on thy holy mountain?
The man of blameless life, who does what is right
and speaks the truth from his heart;
who has no malice on his tongue,
who never wrongs a friend
and tells no tales against his neighbour;
the man who shows his scorn for the worthless
and honours all who fear the Lord;
who swears to his own hurt and does not retract;
who does not put his money out to usury
and takes no bribe against an innocent man.
He who does these things shall never be brought low.'

St Matthew 5,14–16. 'You are light for all the world. A town that stands on a hill cannot be hidden. When a lamp is lit, it is not put under the meal-tub, but on the lamp-stand, where it gives light to everyone in the house. And you, like the lamp, must shed light among your fellows, so that, when they see the good you do, they may give praise to your Father in heaven.'

St John 8,12. 'I am the light of the world. No follower of mine shall wander in the dark; he shall have the light of life.'

PRAYER:

Help us, O God, to rid ourselves of all the things which keep us from being good examples of the faith which we profess.

Help us
Never to demand standards from others which we never even attempt to live up to ourselves;
Never to contradict with our lives that which we say with our lips;
Never to be one thing to people's face and another behind their back.

Help us
Never to make a promise and then to break it because it is difficult to keep;
Never to do anything dishonourable, either to avoid trouble or to make gain;
Never to be disloyal to a friend or untrue to a loved one.

Help us
Not to be the kind of people who are always remembering their rights and always forgetting their duties;
Not to be the kind of people who want to get everything out of life and to put nothing into it;
Not to be the kind of people who do not care what happens to others so long as they are all right.

Help us
Never to teach or to persuade anyone to do a wrong thing;
Never to give an example which will make it easier for someone else to go wrong;
Never to laugh at anyone else's belief, and never to hide our own. *Amen.*

(*William Barclay*)

HYMNS: *Tell out, my soul, the greatness of the Lord*
Ye that know the Lord is gracious

18

BREVITY

Aim: 'Let thy speech be short, comprehending much in few words.'
(*Ecclesiasticus 32.8*)

The more you say, the less people remember.
The fewer the words, the greater the profit.
(*Fénelon*)

The fewer words, the better prayer.
(*Luther*)

Brevity is the soul of wit.
(*Shakespeare, Hamlet Act 11, Scene 2*)

Illustration:
Some time ago all government offices in Washington were circulated with the following list which had no explanation, but speaks for itself:

Lord's Prayer: 57 words (*St Matthew 6,9–13*)
Twenty Third Psalm: 121 words
Gettysburg Address: 264 words
Ten Commandments: 315 words (*Exodus 20,3–17*)
U.S. Department of Agriculture order on the price of cabbages: 15,629 words.

The Gettysburg Address was delivered by Abraham Lincoln at the Dedication of the National Cemetery at Gettysburg on 19 November 1863. It begins and ends thus:

'Fourscore and seven years ago our fathers brought forth upon this continent a new nation, conceived in liberty, and dedicated to the proposition that all men are created equal. Now we are engaged in a great civil war, testing whether that nation, or any nation so conceived and so dedicated can long endure . . .

. . . We here highly resolve that the dead shall not have died in vain, that this nation, under God, shall have a new birth of freedom; and that government of the people, by the people, and for the people, shall not perish from the earth.'

A man is not wise because he has much to say. The wise man is he who is patient, fearless and free from hatred.

A man is not wise because he knows many verses. He who knows little of the law but lives it himself, is called righteous.

(*Buddhist*)

READING:

Psalm 19.

'The heavens tell out the glory of God,
the vault of heaven reveals his handiwork.
One day speaks to another,
night with night shares its knowledge,
  and this without speech or language
  or sound of any voice.
Their music goes out through all the earth,
their words reach to the end of the world.
In them a tent is fixed for the sun,
who comes out like a bridegroom from his wedding canopy,
rejoicing like a strong man to run his race.
  His rising is at one end of the heavens,
  his circuit touches their farthest ends;
  and nothing is hidden from his heat.
The law of the Lord is perfect and revives the soul.
  The Lord's instruction never fails,
  and makes the simple wise.
The precepts of the Lord are right and rejoice the heart.
  The commandment of the Lord shines clear
  and gives light to the eyes.
The fear of the Lord is pure and abides for ever.
The Lord's decrees are true and righteous every one,
more to be desired than gold, pure gold in plenty,
  sweeter than syrup or honey from the comb.
  It is these that give thy servant warning,
  and he who keeps them wins a great reward.
Who is aware of his unwitting sins?
Cleanse me of any secret fault.
Hold back thy servant also from sins of self-will,
  lest they get the better of me.
  Then I shall be blameless
and innocent of any great transgression.
May all that I say and think be acceptable to thee,
  O Lord, my rock and my redeemer.'

PRAYER:

O Lord, we beseech thee to bless and prosper us, gathered here together this day. Grant us reasonableness in all our dealings with each other. Make us large-hearted in helping and generous in criticizing. Keep us from unkind words and unkind silence. Make us quick to understand the needs and feelings of others, and grant that, living in the brightness of thy presence, we may bring thy sunshine into cloudy places, like true followers of Jesus Christ, our Lord. *Amen.*

HYMNS: *God be in my head, and in my understanding*
O thou who camest from above

19

GOD

Aim: The great forgotten truth about God is that he is unknown. Therefore it should be obvious that the way to serve him is not obvious. People always want simplicities, but every simplicity totters on the brink of being so simple as to lie; Christians suffer from too many attempts to make plain what is not plain. There is no interpretation of Christian faith that is not limited; and that means that some aspect of truth eludes every definition, and even more truths elude every practical conclusion.

(*The Revd. Alan Overell, Church Times, June 8, 1984*)

'God is both immanent and imminent, that is, he is both indwelling and transcendental, and yet, God's transcendentalism is only an extension of his immanence.'

'Who beholds me formulates it not, and who formulates me beholds me not.'

(*Muslim*)

'You Lord are near, yet we climb a palm tree to see you.'

(*Kabir*)

Illustration:
(Merlin is trying to explain to the child Arthur why life often appears to be unfair.)

Once upon a time the prophet Elijah went on a journey with the Rabbi Jachanan. They walked all day, and at nightfall they came to the humble cottage of a poor man, whose only treasure was a cow. The poor man ran out of his cottage, and his wife ran too, to welcome the strangers for the night and to offer them all the simple hospitality which they were able to give in straitened circumstances. Elijah and the Rabbi were entertained with plenty of the cow's milk, sustained with home-made bread and butter, and were put to sleep in the best bed while their kindly hosts lay down before the kitchen fire. But in the morning, the poor man's cow was dead.

Elijah and the Rabbi Jachanan walked all the next day, and came that evening to the house of a very wealthy merchant, whose hospitality they craved. The merchant was cold and proud, and all that he would do for the prophet and his companion was to lodge them in a cowshed and feed them on bread and water. In the morning, however, Elijah thanked him very much for what he had done, and sent for a mason to repair one of his walls, which happened to be falling down, as a return for his kindness.

The Rabbi Jachanan, unable to keep silence any longer, begged the holy man to explain the meaning of his dealings with human beings.

'In regard to the poor man who received us so hospitably,' replied the prophet, 'it was decreed that his wife was to die that night, but in reward for his goodness, God took the cow instead of the wife. I repaired the wall of the rich miser because a chest of gold was concealed near the place, and if the miser had repaired the wall himself, he would have discovered the treasure. Say not therefore to the Lord: 'What doest thou?' But say in your heart: 'Must not the Lord of all the earth do right?'

(*T. H. White, The Once and Future King, Fontana/Collins, 1981*)

READINGS:

Isaiah 6,1–4. 'In the year of King Uzziah's death I saw the Lord seated on a throne, high and exalted, and the skirt of his robe filled the temple. About him were attendant seraphim, and each had six wings; one pair covered his face and one pair his feet, and one pair was spread in flight. They were calling ceaselessly to one another,

Holy, holy, holy is the Lord of Hosts:
the whole earth is full of his glory.'

or

Revelation 4.1–11. 'After this I looked, and there before my eyes was a door opened in heaven; and the voice that I had first heard speaking to me like a trumpet said, "Come up here, and I will show you what must happen hereafter." At once I was caught up by the Spirit. There in heaven stood a throne, and on the throne sat one whose appearance was like the gleam of jasper and cornelian; and round the throne was a rainbow, bright as an emerald. In a circle about this throne were twenty-four other thrones, and on them sat twenty-four elders, robed in white and wearing crowns of gold. From the throne went out flashes of lightning and peals of thunder. Burning before the throne were seven flaming torches, the seven spirits of God, and in front of it stretched what seemed a sea of glass, like a sheet of ice.

In the centre, round the throne itself, were four living creatures, covered with eyes, in front and behind. The first creature was like a lion, the second like an ox, the third had a human face, the fourth was like an eagle in flight. The four living creatures, each of them with six wings, had eyes all over, inside and out; and by day and by night without a pause they sang:

"Holy, holy, holy is God the sovereign Lord of all,
who was, and is, and is to come!"

As often as the living creatures give glory and honour and thanks to the One who sits on the throne, who lives for ever and ever, the twenty-four elders fall down before the One who sits on the throne and worship him who lives for ever and ever; and as they lay their crowns before the throne they cry:

"Thou art worthy, O Lord our God, to receive glory and honour and power, because thou didst create all things; by thy will they were created, and have their being!"

or

St Matthew 18.20. 'For where two or three are gathered together in my name there am I in the midst of them.'

or

St John 1,1–5 and 10–14. 'When all things began, the Word already was. The Word dwelt with God, and what God was, the Word was. The Word, then, was with God at the beginning, and through him all things came to be; no single thing was created without him. All that came to be was alive with his life, and that life was the light of men. The light shines on in the dark, and the darkness has never quenched it . . .

He was in the world; but the world, though it owed its being to him, did not recognize him. He entered his own realm, and his own would not receive him. But to all who did receive him, to those who have yielded him their allegiance, he gave the right to become children of God, not born of any human stock, or by the fleshly desire of a human father, but the offspring of God himself. So the Word became flesh; he came to dwell among us, and we saw his glory, such glory as befits the Father's only Son, full of grace and truth.'

or

1 Corinthians 3.16 & 17. 'Surely you know that you are God's temple, where the Spirit of God dwells. Anyone who destroys God's temple will himself be destroyed by God, because the temple of God is holy; and that temple you are.'

or

'. . . And I have felt
A presence that disturbs me with the joy
Of elevated thoughts; a sense sublime
of something far more deeply interfused,
Whose dwelling is the light of setting suns
And the round ocean and the living air,
And the blue sky, and the mind of man.'

(*Lines composed a few miles above Tintern Abbey, Wordsworth*)

PRAYERS:

O Lord of light, whose glory we feel amid the darkness of our thought, we would speak with thee in lowly prayer, but we cannot name thee with a fit and holy name. Where art thou, O thou living God, that we may join all wise and blessed souls in serving thee? Thou art too near for our eye to see thee, too far for our outstretched mind to reach; yet is thy presence even in our midst; and along the pathway of our life, and the wanderings of our hearts, and the transit of our days, we are alone unchangeably with thee.

(*James Martineau*)

O Lord, the Scripture says: 'There is a time for silence and a time for speech', Saviour, teach me the silence of humility, the silence of wisdom, the silence of love, the silence of perfection, the silence that speaks without words, the silence of faith.

Lord teach me to silence my own heart that I may listen to

the gentle movement of the Holy Spirit within me and sense the depths which are of God. *Amen.*

(*Frankfurt Prayer – sixteenth century, translated by B.G.*)

O Lord! Increase my astonishment in Thee!

(*Bahai*)

HYMNS: *O worship the King all glorious above*
Immortal, invisible, God only wise

20

IMITATION

Aim: 'A person will never achieve real greatness simply by imitating another.'

'The worth of a state, in the long run, is the worth of the individuals composing it.'

(*John Stuart Mill*)

'Voyager upon life's sea: –
To yourself be true,
And whatever your lot may be,
Paddle your own canoe.'

(*Edward R. Philpots, Paddle Your Own Canoe*)

Illustration:

A man found an eagle's egg and put it in the nest of a backyard hen. The eaglet hatched with the brood of chicks and grew up with them.

All his life the eagle did what the backyard chickens did, thinking he was a backyard chicken. He scratched the earth for worms and insects. He clucked and cackled. And he would thrash his wings and fly a few feet into the air like the chickens. After all, that is how a chicken is supposed to fly, isn't it?

Years passed and the eagle grew very old. One day he saw a magnificent bird far above him in the cloudless sky. It floated in graceful majesty among the powerful wind currents, with scarcely a beat of its strong golden wings.

The old eagle looked up in awe. 'Who is that?' he said to his neighbour.

'That is the eagle, the king of birds,' said his neighbour. 'But do not give it another thought.'

So the eagle never gave it another thought. He died thinking he was a backyard chicken.

READINGS:

Psalm 15.
'O Lord, who may lodge in thy tabernacle?
Who may dwell on thy holy mountain?
The man of blameless life, who does what is right
and speaks the truth from his heart;
who has no malice on his tongue,
who never wrongs a friend
and tells no tales against his neighbour;
the man who shows his scorn for the worthless
and honours all who fear the Lord;
who swears to his own hurt and does not retract;
who does not put his money out to usury
and takes no bribe against an innocent man.
He who does these things shall never be brought low.'

or

Ephesians 6,13–20. 'Therefore, take up God's armour; then you will be able to stand your ground when things are at their worst, to complete every task and still to stand. Stand firm, I say. Buckle on the belt of truth; for coat of mail put on integrity; let the shoes on your feet be the gospel of peace, to give you firm footing; and, with all these, take up the great shield of faith, with which you will be able to quench all the flaming arrows of the evil one. Take salvation for helmet; for sword, take that which the Spirit gives you – the words that come from God. Give yourselves wholly to prayer and entreaty; pray on every occasion in the power of the Spirit. To this end keep watch and persevere, always interceding for all God's people; and pray for me that I may be granted the right words when I open my mouth, and may boldly and freely make known his hidden purpose, for which I am an ambassador – in chains. Pray that I may speak of it boldly, as it is my duty to speak.'

or

'This above all: to thine own self be true,
And it must follow, as the night the day.
Thou canst not then be false to any man.'
(*William Shakespeare, Hamlet I.iii.58*)

PRAYER:

O God help us to remember
That you gave us life,
and that it is not ours to do with as we like.
That life comes to an end,
and that we must not waste it when we have it.
Help us,
To use life wisely and not foolishly;
To use life generously and not selfishly;
To use life strenuously and not lazily;
To use life with discipline and not with self-indulgence;
To use life in the constant memory that one
day we shall give account of it to you. *Amen.*

HYMNS: *Stand up! Stand up for Jesus*
Lord of all power, I give you my will

21

CHRISTIAN UNITY

Aim: How much more effective the witness of the Church would be if it was not handicapped by so many unhappy divisions.

'In Unity there is strength.'

Illustration:
A farmer whose sons were always quarrelling tried to point out to them that if only they would work together, the farm would flourish all the more, and they would all be better off. The father also pointed out to them that unless they stood together an enemy could easily

take advantage of their weakness. But the sons took no notice of the old man's advice. So he decided to give them an object lesson. He summoned his sons into his presence and carefully laid twelve slender sticks, one by one, on the table in front of him. Then, taking some string, he tied the sticks into a bundle. The father invited each of his sons to step forward, pick up the bundle and break it in two. Not one of them succeeded in doing so. The old man picked up the bundle, undid the string and once again, placed the sticks one by one in a row on the surface of the table. Turning to the youngest of his sons, he handed him the sticks one at a time and asked him to break them. This he did with the greatest of ease.

(*Aesop*)

READINGS:

1 Corinthians, 3–5. 'Can you not see that while there is jealousy and strife among you, you are living on the purely human level of your lower nature? When one says, "I am Paul's man", and another, "I am for Apollos", are you not all too human?

After all, what is Apollos? What is Paul? We are simply God's agents in bringing you to the faith.'

or

1 Corinthians 12,4–13. 'There are varieties of gifts, but the same Spirit. There are varieties of service, but the same Lord. There are many forms of work, but all of them, in all men, are the work of the same God. In each of us the Spirit is manifested in one particular way, for some useful purpose. One man, through the Spirit, has the gift of wise speech, while another, by the power of the same Spirit, can put the deepest knowledge into words. Another, by the same Spirit, is granted faith; another, by the one Spirit, gifts of healing, and another miraculous powers; another has the gift of prophecy, and another ability to distinguish true spirits from false; yet another has the gift of ecstatic utterance of different kinds, and another the ability to interpret it. But all these gifts are the work of one and the same Spirit, distributing them separately to each individual at will.

For Christ is like a single body with its many limbs and organs, which, many as they are, together make up one body. For indeed we were all brought into one body by baptism, in the one Spirit, whether we are Jews or Greeks, whether slaves or free men, and that one Holy Spirit was poured out for all of us to drink.'

PRAYERS:

O God, the Father of our Lord Jesus Christ, our only Saviour, the Prince of Peace; Give us grace seriously to lay to heart the great dangers we are in by our unhappy divisions. Take away all hatred and prejudice, and whatsoever else may hinder us from godly union and concord: that as there is but one Body and one Spirit, and one hope of our calling, one Lord, one faith, one baptism, one God and Father of us all, so we may henceforth be all of one heart and of one soul, united in one holy bond of truth and peace, of faith and charity, and may with one mind and one mouth glorify thee, through Jesus Christ our Lord. *Amen.*

Father,
who hast made all men in thy likeness and lovest all whom thou has made, suffer not our family to separate itself from thee by building barriers of race and colour. As thy Son our Saviour was born of a Hebrew mother, but rejoiced in the faith of a Syrian woman and of a Roman soldier, welcomed the Greeks who sought him, and suffered a man from Africa to carry his cross, so teach us to regard the members of all races as fellow-heirs in the kingdom of Jesus Christ our Lord. *Amen.*

(*The Oxford Book of Prayer*)

HYMNS: *The Church's one foundation*
In Christ there is no east or west

22

EVOLUTION

Aim: When we consider even the smallest of the creatures, we begin to realize how little we know about nature and creation.

Illustration:
Consider the species of beetle called Oncideres. This species of beetle is not new, but it qualifies as a modern Wonder because of the

exceedingly modern questions raised for evolutionary biologists by the three consecutive thoughts that pop into the mind of the female.

Her first thought is for a mimosa tree, which she finds and climbs, ignoring all other kinds of trees. Her second thought is for laying eggs, which she does by crawling out on a limb, cutting a longitudinal slit with her mandible and depositing her eggs beneath the slit. Her third and last thought concerns the welfare of her offspring; beetle larvae cannot survive in live wood, so she moves back a foot or so and cuts a neat girdle all round the limb, through the bark. It takes her eight hours to do this cabinetwork.

The limb dies from the girdling, falls to the ground in the next breeze, the larvae feed and grow into the next generation, and the questions lie there unanswered.

How did these three linked thoughts emerge together in her evolution? Is this mindless behaviour, or is it possible for the tiny brain of a beetle to contain thoughts and bits of awareness exactly like ours, just three microscopic thoughts popping into her mind, always in the right order? And how did the mimosa tree enter the picture in its evolution?

Left to themselves, unpruned, mimosa trees have a life expectancy of 25 to 30 years. Pruned each year, which is what the beetle's girdling accomplishes, the tree can flourish for a century. The mimosa–beetle relationship is an elegant example of symbiotic partnership. It is good for us to have around such creatures as this insect and its partner tree, for they keep reminding us how little we know about nature.

(*Lewis Thomas, Seven Wonders of My World. Readers Digest, June 1984*)

READING:

Job 38,1–12.

'Then the Lord answered Job out of the tempest:
Who is this whose ignorant words
cloud my design in darkness?
Brace yourself and stand up like a man;
I will ask questions, and you shall answer.
Where were you when I laid the earth's foundations?
Tell me, if you know and understand.
Who settled its dimensions? Surely you should know.
Who stretched his measuring-line over it?
On what do its supporting pillars rest?
Who set its corner-stone in place,
when the morning stars sang together

and all the sons of God shouted aloud?
Who watched over the birth of the sea,
when it burst in flood from the womb? –
when I wrapped it in a blanket of cloud
and cradled it in fog,
when I established its bounds,
fixing its doors and bars in place,
and said, "Thus far shall you come and no further,
and here your surging waves shall halt."
In all your life have you ever called up the dawn
or shown the morning its place?'

PRAYER:

We thank thee O God, that thou hast given us the enquiring mind to delve into thy laws and search for thy truth. We pray that our reverence may increase with our knowledge, so that we may be led to worship thee with deepening humility and so dedicate ourselves to the fulfilment of thy great purposes for the glory of our Lord and Saviour Jesus Christ. *Amen.*

HYMNS: *O worship the King all glorious above*
All things bright and beautiful

23

POLLUTION

Aim: The writer of the first chapter of the Book of Genesis tells us in verses 27–30 that God gave man the responsibility of ruling over the world. All of us, therefore, are responsible to God for the well being of that part of the world in which we live. We must be careful not to pollute it and be watchful of others who may treat it carelessly.

Illustration:
'Mummy, Oh Mummy, what's this pollution
That everyone's talking about?'
'Pollution's the mess that the country is in,
That we'd all be far better without.
It's factories belching their fumes in the air,
And the beaches all covered with tar,
Now throw all those sweet papers into the bushes
Before we get back in the car.'

'Mummy, Oh Mummy, who makes pollution,
And why don't they stop if it's bad?'
' 'Cos people like that just don't think about others,
They don't think at all, I might add.
They spray all the crops and they poison the flowers,
And wipe out the birds and the bees,
Now there's a good place we could dump that old mattress
Right out of sight in the trees.'

'Mummy, Oh Mummy, what is going to happen
If all the pollution goes on?'
'Well the world will end up like a second-hand junk-yard,
With all of its treasures quite gone.
The fields will be littered with plastics and tins,
The streams will be covered with foam,
Now throw those two pop bottles over the hedge,
Save us from carting them home.'

'But Mummy, Oh Mummy, if I throw the bottles,
Won't that be polluting the wood?'
'Nonsense! that isn't the same thing at all,
You just shut up and be good.
If you're going to start getting silly ideas
I'm taking you home right away,
'Cos pollution is something that other folk do,
We're just enjoying our day.'

(*Source Unknown*)

READING:

Genesis 1 and 2,1–4. 'In the beginning of creation, when God made heaven and earth, the earth was without form and void, with darkness over the face of the abyss, and a mighty wind that swept over the surface of the waters. God said, "Let there be light", and there was light; and God saw that the light was good, and he separated light from darkness. He called the light day, and the darkness night. So evening came, and morning came, the first day.

God said, "Let there be a vault between the waters, to separate water from water." So God made the vault, and separated the water under the vault from the water above it, and so it was; and God called the vault heaven. Evening came, and morning came, a second day.

God said, "Let the waters under heaven be gathered into one place, so that dry land may appear"; and so it was. God called the dry land earth, and the gathering of the waters he called seas; and God saw that it was good. Then God said, "Let the earth produce fresh growth, let there be on the earth plants bearing seed, fruit-trees bearing fruit each with seed according to its kind." So it was; the earth yielded fresh growth, plants bearing seed according to their kind and trees bearing fruit each with seed according to its kind; and God saw that it was good. Evening came, and morning came, a third day.

God said, "Let there be lights in the vault of heaven to separate day from night, and let them serve as signs both for festivals and for seasons and years. Let them also shine in the vault of heaven to give light on earth." So it was; God made the two great lights, the greater to govern the day and the lesser to govern the night; and with them he made the stars. God put these lights in the vault of heaven to give light on earth, to govern day and night, and separate light from darkness; and God saw that it was good. Evening came, and morning came, a fourth day.

God said, "Let the waters teem with countless living creatures, and let birds fly above the earth across the vault of heaven." God then created great sea-monsters and all living creatures that move and swarm in the waters, according to their kind, and every kind of bird; and God saw that it was good. So he blessed them and said, "Be fruitful and increase, fill the waters of the seas; and let the birds increase on land." Evening came, and morning came, a fifth day.

God said, "Let the earth bring forth living creatures, according to their kind: cattle, reptiles, and wild animals, all according to their kind." So it was; God made wild animals, cattle, and all reptiles, each according to its kind; and he saw that it was good. Then God said, "Let us make man in our image and likeness to rule the fish in the sea, the birds of heaven, the cattle, all wild animals on earth, and all reptiles that crawl upon the earth." So God created man in his own image; in the image of God he created him; male and female he created them. God blessed them and said to them, "Be fruitful and increase, fill the earth and subdue it, rule over the fish in the sea, the birds of heaven, and every living thing that moves upon the earth." God also said, "I give you all plants that bear seed everywhere on earth, and every tree bearing fruit which yields seed; they shall be yours for food. All green plants I give for food to the wild animals, to all the birds of heaven, and to all reptiles on earth, every living creature." So it was; and God saw all that he had made, and it was very good. Evening came, and morning came, a sixth day.

Thus heaven and earth were completed with all their mighty throng. On the sixth day God completed all the work he had been doing, and on the seventh day he ceased from all his work. God blessed the seventh day and made it holy, because on that day he ceased from all the work he had set himself to do.

This is the story of the making of heaven and earth when they were created.'

PRAYER:

O God, we thank thee for this earth, our home; for the wide sky and the blessed sun, for the salt sea and the running water, for the everlasting hills and the never resting winds, for trees and the common grass underfoot. We thank thee for our senses by which we hear the songs of birds, and see the splendour of the summer fields, and taste of autumn fruits, and rejoice in the feel of snow, and smell the breath of Spring. Grant us a heart wide open to all this beauty, and save our souls from being so blind that we pass unseeing when even the common thorn bush is aflame with thy glory; O God, our Creator, who livest and reignest forever. *Amen.*

(*Walter Rauschenbach*)

HYMNS: *All things bright and beautiful*
All creatures of our God and King

Tuesday

5

24

SELF DISCIPLINE

Aim: Whoever we are, however accomplished we may be, however strong we may think we are, we must be constantly vigilant because we all have weaknesses, and it is through these weaknesses that alcohol and drugs can penetrate and destroy.

Illustration:
St Mark's was a very fashionable church. With its lovely setting alongside a park and abutting a glorious river, it was always in great demand for weddings.

The Vicar was a kind man, and allowed old Jack to shelter in the furnace room during the cold weather. In return, when he was sober, Jack did a bit of tidying up around the graveyard and swept away the confetti after weddings. Sometimes the Vicar gave Jack a pound or two for his labours, but was reluctant to give him more because Jack simply spent it all on drink.

One Saturday guests began arriving for a wedding, and it was clear from the expensive cars in which they arrived that it was a very special occasion. The Vicar was standing at the West door smiling a warm welcome to all and sundry, but clearly, from the way he was looking at his watch and the worried frown which constantly returned to crease his brow, he had something on his mind. As the finger of the church clock crept towards noon, the Vicar, catching sight of Jack lurking with his brush behind a grave stone, went up to him and said,

'Have you seen any sight of the organist?'

'No sir, I have not,' came the reply.

'Oh dear,' groaned the Vicar, 'I fear I have made an awful slip up. With so many weddings going on, I must have forgotten to inform him about this one. Whatever am I going to do? The ceremony will be ruined! The family will never forgive me, and I shall be the talking point of the whole town. And there isn't time to do anything about it.'

'Well!' said Jack. 'Perhaps one of the guests can play. Why don't you go in and make an appeal?'

'I cannot do that Jack,' replied the Vicar, with desperation in his voice. 'The organ is a four manual with dozens of stops, and what is more, the voluntaries chosen by the bride could not be more difficult.'

'What are they?' queried Jack.

The Vicar handed him the 'Order of Service' and simply pointed. Jack scanned the sheet and then said,

'I think I could cope with all that. Would you like me to play?'

'What!' exclaimed the Vicar, 'You, Jack? I didn't have the faintest idea that you were an organist!'

'Well that's understandable sir – especially since you have never heard me play.'

'Look,' said the Vicar, 'the bride will be here in minutes; if you think you can manage it, please go in now. Use the vestry door, otherwise the congregation will be wondering what is happening.'

Jack shuffled off in the direction of the Vestry and the Vicar resumed his position at the door. He had never felt so nervous and helpless in his life. 'Jack!' he muttered to himself. 'What on earth could Jack do?' And then he heard it – music from the organ! Music the like of which he had never heard before. Superb music! Never had the organ of St Mark's been played with such skill and sensitivity. Hymns, anthem, voluntaries, followed one another with ever increasing beauty.

After the service, the Vicar went in search of Jack and found him carefully brushing away the confetti.

'Jack,' said the Vicar, 'thank you from the bottom of my heart. You saved the day! Here is your fee. Take it, and put that brush away.'

Jack took his fee and thanked the Vicar and continued with his brushing.

'Tell me,' said the Vicar, very gently, 'who are you Jack?'

There was no reply. The Vicar did not press his question because he could see that Jack was sobbing quietly to himself.

READINGS:

Proverbs 23,29–35.

'Whose is the misery? Whose the remorse?
Whose are the quarrels and the anxiety?
Who get the bruises without knowing why?
Whose eyes are bloodshot?
Those who linger late over their wine,
those who are always trying some new spiced liquor.
Do not gulp down the wine, the strong red wine,
when the droplets form on the side of the cup;
in the end it will bite like a snake
and sting like a cobra.
Then your eyes see strange sights,
your wits and your speech are confused;
you become like a man tossing out at sea,
like one who clings to the top of the rigging;
you say, 'If it lays me flat, what do I care?

If it brings me to the ground, what of it?
As soon as I wake up,
I shall turn to it again.'

or

1 Peter 5,8–10. 'Awake! be on the alert! Your enemy the devil, like a roaring lion, prowls round looking for someone to devour. Stand up to him, firm in faith, and remember that your brother Christians are going through the same kinds of suffering while they are in the world. And the God of all grace, who called you into his eternal glory in Christ, will himself, after your brief suffering, restore, establish, and strengthen you on a firm foundation.'

PRAYERS:

Almighty and everlasting God, who for the well-being of our earthly life hast put into our hearts wholesome desires of body and spirit: Mercifully increase and establish in us, we beseech thee, the grace of holy discipline and healthy self-control; that we may fulfil our desires by the means which thou hast appointed, and for the ends thou ordainest; through Jesus Christ our Lord. *Amen.*

O God, give us:
Courage always to do the right;
Strength always to resist the wrong;
Perseverance never to give up;
Respect for ourselves and love for others
for Jesus sake. *Amen.*

HYMNS: ×*O Jesus I have promised*×
Forth in thy name, O Lord, I go

94
96

25

BE PREPARED!

Aim: Procrastination is the thief of time.

(*Edward Young*)

The regiment which has not mastered its manoeuvres on the training ground cannot hope to do so on the field of battle.

Illustration:

One of the most ancient legends of Wales tells us that long, long ago what is now the Dovey estuary was a fertile plain with many prosperous villages, and known as Cantre'r Gwaelod. This plain was protected from the sea by a vast embankment made of earth and stone. Along this embankment were a series of watch towers, each under the care of a warden. The largest of these towers was situated at the centre, and was occupied by Prince Seithenyn, the chief warden of the Royal Embankment.

Prince Seithenyn was one of the most popular and generous figures of his day. Travellers were always welcome at his gates, and given royal treatment. Banquet followed banquet and the wine flowed freely. From time to time Prince Seithenyn received reports from his wardens that sections of the embankment were showing signs of erosion and that certain sluice gates were showing evidence of decay, but Seithenyn simply laughed and shrugged his shoulders and assured his wardens that they had nothing to worry about; the embankment had lasted for hundreds of years and would very likely last a few hundred more. Sometimes an anxious warden would succeed in persuading Seithenyn to visit a crumbling section, or to view a rotting sluice gate, but apart from a vague promise to look into the matter, Seithenyn never took any effective action.

And then one night it happened. Long and heavy rainfall in the Cambrian Mountains caused the River Dovey to burst its banks, and this coincided with the high Spring tides and a strong following wind. The long neglected embankment attacked by the swirling flood waters of the Dovey on one side and the remorseless pounding waves of the open sea on the other, could not withstand the strain. Long neglected sluice gates collapsed and eroded sections of earth and stone simply dissolved away.

When morning dawned, all trace of the embankment and its watchtowers had disappeared. And the fertile plain together with its villages and farmsteads had sunk beneath the waters of the sea.

Today, there is nothing to remind the traveller, as he stands gazing across the waters of the Dovey Estuary, that beneath the waves people once lived and farmed and worshipped in their village churches. Except perhaps for those with keen ears, because down through the centuries many have claimed to have heard the bells of those churches ringing under the waters!

All this happened because Prince Seithenyn through sheer neglect was not ready when an emergency appeared.

READING:

St Matthew 25,1–13. 'When that day comes, the kingdom of Heaven will be like this. There were ten girls, who took their lamps and went out to meet the bridegroom. Five of them were foolish, and five prudent; when the foolish ones took their lamps, they took no oil with them, but the others took flasks of oil with their lamps. As the bridegroom was late in coming they all dozed off to sleep. But at midnight a cry was heard: "Here is the bridegroom. Come out to meet him." With that the girls all got up and trimmed their lamps. The foolish said to the prudent, "Our lamps are going out; give us some of your oil." "No," they said; "there will never be enough for us both. You had better go to the shop and buy some for yourselves." While they were away the bridegroom arrived; those who were ready went in with him to the wedding; and the door was shut. And then the other five came back. "Sir, sir," they cried, "open the door for us." But he answered, "I declare, I do not know you." Keep awake then; for you never know the day or the hour.'

PRAYERS:

O God, help us to use life as it ought to be used,
Help us always to remember,
That you gave us life
and that it is not ours to do with as we like;
That life comes to an end,
and we must not waste it when we have it;
That we cannot tell what a day will bring us,
And so we must not put things off until tomorrow
in case tomorrow never comes. *Amen.*

Help us,
To use life wisely and not foolishly;
To use life generously and not selfishly;

To use life strenuously and not lazily;
To use life with discipline and not with self-indulgence;
To use life in the constant memory that one day
  we shall give account of it to you.
To that end help us always to walk with Jesus
who is the Lord of all good life who came to
give us life and life more abundantly. *Amen.*

HYMNS: *Ye servants of the Lord*
Sleepers, wake! the watch-cry pealeth

26

SIN

Aim: The Greek word for 'sin' is HAMARTIA and HAMARTANEIN is the Greek verb for 'to sin'. In classical Greek HAMARTEIN was a term used in archery meaning 'to fall short of' as when an archer shooting at a target falls short of it. 'To sin' means to fall short of a standard, and in particular, the standard of your own conscience. But beware and heed the truth enshrined in the story below.

'The will needs to be disciplined, for it tells the body what acts to perform. Our intellects give us our targets, but it is our wills that shoot the arrows. The disciplined will shows its strength in the way it governs the passions, emotions and senses. Weak wills are usual among those who have no ideals, no goal in life, those whose decisions are wholly capricious, who are influenced by human respect and the bad example of others, who decide what to do by copying what everybody else is doing.'

(*Bishop Fulton Sheen*)

Illustration:
Two men once visited a holy man to ask his advice.

'We have done wrong actions,' they said, 'and our consciences are troubled. What must we do to be forgiven?'

'Tell me of your wrong-doings, my sons,' said the old man.

The first man said, 'I committed a great and terrible sin.'

The second man said, 'I have done a number of wrong things, but they are quite small and unimportant.'

The holy man looked at each of them and said,

'Go and bring me a stone for each of your misdeeds.'

The first man set off and searched around until he found a huge boulder which matched the size of his misdeed. He heaved the boulder on to his shoulder and staggered back with it to the holy man.

The second man gathered a number of small pebbles, and placing them in a bag, also brought them back to the holy man.

'Now,' said the holy man, 'go and put them back exactly where you found them.'

The first man shouldered his great boulder again, and staggered back to the place where he had found it.

The second man, however, could only remember a few of the places where he had picked up his pebbles. He came back saying that the task was too difficult.

'Sins are like these stones,' said the holy man. 'If a man has committed a great sin, it lies like a heavy stone on his conscience; yet if he is truly sorry, he is forgiven and the load of guilt is taken away. But if a man is constantly doing small things that he knows to be wrong, he does not feel any great load of guilt, and so he is not sorry, and remains a sinner. So you see, my sons, it is as important to avoid little sins as big ones.'

(*Slav folk-tale*)

READINGS:

Ephesians 4,23–5,5. 'You must be made new in mind and spirit, and put on the new nature of God's creating, which shows itself in the just and devout life called for by the truth.

Then throw off falsehood; speak the truth to each other, for all of us are the parts of one body.

If you are angry, do not let anger lead you into sin; do not let sunset find you still nursing it; leave no loop-hole for the devil.

The thief must give up stealing, and instead work hard and honestly with his own hands, so that he may have something to share with the needy.

No bad language must pass your lips, but only what is good and helpful to the occasion, so that it brings a blessing to those who hear it. And do not grieve the Holy Spirit of God, for that Spirit is the seal with which you were marked for the day of our final liberation. Have done with spite and passion, all angry shouting and cursing, and bad feeling of every kind.

Be generous to one another, tender-hearted, forgiving one another as God in Christ forgave you.

In a word, as God's dear children, try to be like him, and live in love as Christ loved you, and gave himself up on your behalf as an offering and sacrifice whose fragrance is pleasing to God.

Fornication and indecency of any kind, or ruthless greed, must not be so much as mentioned among you, as befits the people of God. No coarse, stupid, or flippant talk; these things are out of place; you should rather be thanking God. For be very sure of this: no one given to fornication or indecency, or the greed which makes an idol of gain, has any share in the kingdom of Christ and of God.'

Romans 7,14–25.

PRAYERS:

For
All that we ought to have thought and have not thought,
All that we ought to have said and have not said,
All that we ought to have done and have not done:
For
All that we ought not to have thought and yet have thought,
All that we ought not to have spoken and yet have spoken,
All that we ought not to have done and yet have done;
For thoughts, words and deeds, pray we, O God, for forgiveness,
And repent with penance.

(*Zoroaster c.600 B.C., The Zendavesta*)

Almighty God, who seest that we have no power of ourselves to help ourselves; keep us both outwardly in our bodies, and inwardly in our souls; that we may be defended from all adversities which may happen to the body, and from all evil thoughts which may assault and hurt the soul: through Jesus Christ our Lord. *Amen.*

(*Gregorian Sacramentary*)

HYMNS: *Soldiers of Christ, arise*
Be thou my guardian and my guide

27

LUKE-WARM

Aim: 'You will only get out of a bucket what you put into it.' When our Church, our Societies, our Clubs, our Unions begin to falter and slump, it is no good simply shaking our heads and moaning about matters. We must be prepared to do something, such as contributing our time and our energies.

Illustration:

A minister in the Middle West of America had been working as hard as he could to revive and renew his congregation. All his efforts had been met by the dead hand of apathy. There were the usual financial complaints, there were complaints about the lack of social life in the church, there were complaints about him and his preaching. It was this, and his experiments, according to his critics, that was going to lead rapidly to the death of the church.

Exasperated beyond measure, he advertised in the local Press that, next Sunday, there would be held at ten o'clock a burial service for his dead church. There had not been such a congregation for years! Human curiosity remains insatiable. When the place was packed from floor to ceiling, the minister gravely conducted the obsequies. Even the hymns were the favourites for such occasions – 'Abide with me' and 'Lead, kindly Light'. In the very centre of the church was one of those huge American coffins, open for all to see.

After the blessing, the minister, playing on the intensity of human curiosity, invited all his congregation to file past the coffin to pay their last respects. He knew as well as anyone else that everybody wanted to see what it contained. The whole congregation filed past one by one. Their expressions were many and varied as they left the church. When they looked into this exquisite product of the coffin-maker's art, there on the silk lining was a large mirror which reflected their own image.

(*As told by Lynda Jones*)

READINGS:

Philippians 2,1–18. 'If then our common life in Christ yields anything to stir the heart, any loving consolation, any sharing of the Spirit, any warmth of affection or compassion, fill my cup of happiness by thinking and feeling alike, with the same love for one another, the same turn of mind, and a common care for unity. Rivalry and personal vanity should have no place among you, but you should humbly reckon others better than yourselves. You must look to each other's interest and not merely to your own.

Let your bearing towards one another arise out of your life in Christ Jesus. For the divine nature was his from the first; yet he did not think to snatch at equality with God, but made himself nothing, assuming the nature of a slave. Bearing the human likeness, revealed in human shape, he humbled himself, and in obedience accepted even death – death on a cross. Therefore God raised him to the heights and bestowed on him the name above all names, that at the name of Jesus every knee should bow – in heaven, on earth, and in the depths – and every tongue confess, 'Jesus Christ is Lord', to the glory of God the Father.

So you too, my friends, must be obedient, as always; even more, now that I am away, than when I was with you. You must work out your own salvation in fear and trembling; for it is God who works in you, inspiring both the will and the deed, for his own chosen purpose.

Do all you have to do without complaint or wrangling. Show yourselves guileless and above reproach, faultless children of God in a warped and crooked generation, in which you shine like stars in a dark world and proffer the word of life. Thus you will be my pride on the Day of Christ, proof that I did not run my race in vain, or work in vain. But if my life-blood is to crown that sacrifice which is the offering up of your faith, I am glad of it, and I share my gladness with you all. Rejoice, you no less than I, and let us share our joy.'

1 Peter 4,1–11.

Revelation 3,1–3 and 15 & 16.

PRAYER:

O God, help us to remember,
That you gave us life,
and that it is not ours to do with as we like;
That life comes to an end,
and that we must not waste it when we have it;
That we cannot tell what a day will bring us,
and so we must not put things off until tomorrow in case tomorrow never comes.

Help us,
To use life wisely and not foolishly;
To use life generously and not selfishly;
To use life strenuously and not lazily;
To use life with discipline and not with self-indulgence;
To use life in the constant memory that one day
we shall give account of it to you. *Amen.*

(*William Barclay*)

HYMNS: *O thou who camest from above*
And did those feet in ancient times

28

GOD'S SERVICE

Aim: Teach me, my God and King,
In all things Thee to see;
And what I do in any thing,
To do it as for Thee!

(*George Herbert*)

When a man turns to God desiring to serve him,
God directs his attention to the world and its need.

(*Emil Brunner, The Divine Imperative*)

Illustration:
There was once a builder who had a very wealthy friend. One day the wealthy friend came to the builder and asked him to build him a house. He handed over the plans and explained that he only wanted the very best materials to be used in the construction, and that he must spare no expense.

The builder studied the plans very carefully and said to himself, 'My opportunity has come to make a really fat profit!'

He built the foundations and walls with the cheapest materials he could find, covering them with just a thin show of the best material. The doors and window frames were made of the cheapest stuff artfully made to look like the most expensive wood. And so it went on.

Eventually the house was finished and it looked magnificent. The builder submitted the bill to his wealthy friend who settled it immediately. As the builder turned to go, his friend called him back and said,

'William, I have noticed over the years, how you have worked hard to build fine houses for other people, whilst continuing to live in a small house yourself. I would like you to accept this house from me as a gift. And I hope that you and your wife may be spared to live many happy long years in it.'

You can picture the feelings of that builder, as he watched the doors warp, the windows leak, the ceilings crack and the foundations slip as the years passed by.

READINGS:

St Matthew 7,24–27. 'What then of the man who hears these words of mine and acts upon them? He is like a man who had the sense to build his house on rock. The rain came down, the floods rose, the wind blew, and beat upon that house; but it did not fall, because its foundations were on rock. But what of the man who hears these words of mine and does not act upon them? He is like a man who was foolish enough to build his house on sand. The rain came down, the floods rose, the wind blew, and beat upon that house; down it fell with a great crash.'

1 Corinthians 3,10–17. 'Or again, you are God's building. I am like a skilled master-builder who by God's grace laid the foundation, and someone else is putting up the building. Let each take care how he builds. There can be no other foundation beyond that which is already laid; I mean Jesus Christ himself. If anyone builds on that foundation with gold and silver and fine stone, or with wood, hay, and straw, the work that each man does will at last be brought to light; the day of judgement will expose it. For that day dawns in fire, and the fire will test the worth of each man's work. If a man's building stands, he will be rewarded; if it burns, he will have to bear the loss; and yet he will escape with his life, as one might from a fire. Surely you know that you are God's temple, where the Spirit of God dwells. Anyone who destroys God's temple will himself be destroyed by God, because the temple of God is holy; and that temple you are.'

PRAYER:

O Lord Jesus Christ,
Take our hands, and work with them;
Take our lips and speak through them;
Take our minds, and think with them;
Take our hearts, and set them on fire
With love for Thee and for all mankind:
For Thy sake. *Amen*.

(*Warwick School*)

HYMNS: *Lord of all being I give you my will*
Rise up, O men of God. Have done with lesser things

29

PRAYER

Aim: God helps those who help themselves.

It is not so much that prayer changes things as prayer changes us and we change things.

Pray as if everything depended on God, and act as if everything depended on oneself.

(*St Ignatius Loyola*)

Illustration:
Prolonged torrential rain high up in the mountains caused the river to burst its banks and flood the plain. Roads became impassable, and soon villages and towns were in danger of being swept away. All sorts of emergency services were rushed in to help as a massive rescue operation was launched. The minister of one of the churches had sought refuge at the top of one of his apple trees, and there he prayed to God for help as the water crept higher and higher. As he sat crouched on the top-most bough, a young lad came paddling by in a tiny canoe. When he saw the minister crouched in the apple tree, he paddled towards him and said,

'Would you like a lift? You can squeeze into the space in front of me if you like.'

The minister thanked the boy and said,

'No, thank you, I will be all right. I have faith in God.'

A few minutes later a boat full of survivors floated into view. When they saw the minister, they 'hove to' and offered him a lift to higher ground. But the minister declined, preferring to put his trust in God.

Finally a helicopter flew by. Hovering over the tree, the crew-man lowered a rope ladder and signalled to the minister to climb up. But once again, the minister declined the offer,

'No thanks,' he shouted, 'I have faith in God, and he will save me!'

So the helicopter flew away. The waters continued to rise and the minister, who could not swim, was drowned.

Soon afterwards, he found himself in heaven, standing before the throne of God.

'Tell me Lord,' he said, with a certain reproach in his voice, 'why didn't you save me from drowning? I thought you not only looked after, but also listened to the prayers of those who put their trust in you.'

God replied, 'I always look after my children and I always listen to their prayers. What more could I have done for you? I sent you a canoe, a boat and a helicopter, but you turned them all away.'

READINGS:

St Luke 11,1–4. 'Once, in a certain place, Jesus was at prayer. When he ceased, one of his disciples said, "Lord, teach us to pray, as John taught his disciples." He answered, "When you pray, say,

Father, thy name be hallowed;
Thy kingdom come.
Give us each day our daily bread.
And forgive us our sins,
For we too forgive all who have done us wrong.
And do not bring us to the test."'

St Matthew 7,7–11. 'Ask, and you will receive; seek, and you will find; knock, and the door will be opened. For everyone who asks receives, he who seeks finds, and to him who knocks, the door will be opened.

Is there a man among you who will offer his son a stone when he asks for bread, or a snake when he asks for fish? If you, then, bad as you are, know how to give your children what is good for them, how much more will your heavenly Father give good things to those who ask him.'

St Luke 18,1–8.

PRAYER:

God be in my head,
  And in my understanding:
God be in my eyes,
  And in my looking:
God be in my mouth,
  And in my speaking:
God be in my heart,
  And in my thinking:
God be at my end,
  And at my departing.

O God, give us,
  Serenity to accept what cannot be changed;
  Courage to change what should be changed;
  And wisdom to distinguish the one from the other;
  Through Jesus Christ our Lord. *Amen*.

(*Reinhold Niebuhr*)

HYMNS: *Put thou thy trust in God*
O God, our help in ages past

30

HOPE

Aim: Hope says to us constantly, 'Go on, go on', and leads us thus to the grave.

(*Mme de Maintenon*)

Hope springs eternal in the human breast.

(*Pope – Essay on Man*)

Hope is one of the three great pillars of the Christian faith. It is on hope, along with faith and love, that the whole Christian faith is founded.

(*William Barclay*)

Illustration:

After having seen a film on Paris, the young Greek farmer became fired with the ambition of visiting that city and experiencing its delights at first hand. He set himself a target and reckoned that it would take about five years to save the necessary money to cover the return fare for the train journey across Europe and a week's holiday in Paris.

During the next five years he worked hard in his vineyard and olive grove and went without the usual luxuries in order to accumulate the necessary capital. Just as his goal came into sight, his father died, and since the family was poor, the young man felt morally bound to shoulder the expense of the funeral, which meant that most of his savings had to be spent. Undeterred by this set-back, he again applied himself to the goal of saving sufficient money for his Paris visit. Four years passed by and he began to prepare for his holiday, when his youngest sister declared that she and her sweetheart wished to get married. This, of course, meant that a suitable dowry had to be found, and, once again, the Greek farmer decided to forego his Paris trip for the sake of his sister's happiness. He handed over his savings as her marriage dowry.

Yet again he began to save with the same end in view. Five years later, he reached his target, and this time, without interruption, raised his ticket and boarded the train for Paris. As the train ate up the miles, his excitement grew and grew.

'It won't be long now,' he whispered to himself 'before I shall be walking down the Champs Elysee.'

He eagerly ticked off each station on the map which lay spread across his knees, until eventually the train pulled into the last station before Paris. Suddenly he stood up, reached for his case and stepped off the train. Then, crossing to the other platform, he caught the train back to Athens.

When he arrived home, his family were surprised to see him.

'Why' they asked, 'have you returned so soon?'

Shrugging his shoulders and spreading his hands, he smiled and said, 'I cannot give a logical explanation, other than to say that when I arrived at that last station it struck me that if I reached Paris all my hopes would be realized and that I would no longer have anything to hope for.'

READINGS:

1 Corinthians 13. 'I may speak in tongues of men or of angels, but if I am without love, I am a sounding gong or a clanging cymbal. I may have the gift of prophecy, and know every hidden truth; I may have faith strong enough to move mountains; but if I have no love, I am nothing. I may dole out all I possess, or even give my body to be burnt, but if I have no love, I am none the better.

Love is patient; love is kind and envies no one. Love is never boastful, nor conceited, nor rude; never selfish, not quick to take offence. Love keeps no score of wrongs; does not gloat over other men's sins, but delights in the truth. There is nothing love cannot face; there is no limit to its faith, its hope, and its endurance.

Love will never come to an end. Are there prophets? their work will be over. Are there tongues of ecstasy? they will cease. Is there knowledge? it will vanish away; for our knowledge and our prophecy alike are partial, and the partial vanishes when wholeness comes. When I was a child, my speech, my outlook, and my thoughts were all childish. When I grew up, I had finished with childish things. Now we see only puzzling reflections in a mirror, but then we shall see face to face. My knowledge now is partial; then it will be whole, like God's knowledge of men. In a word, there are three things that last for ever: faith, hope, and love; but the greatest of them all is love.'

1 Peter 1,3–5. 'Praise be to the God and Father of our Lord Jesus Christ, who in his mercy gave us new birth into a living hope by the resurrection of Jesus Christ from the dead! The inheritance to which we are born is one that nothing can destroy or spoil or wither. It is kept for you in heaven, and you, because you put your faith in God, are under the protection of his power until salvation comes – the salvation which is even now in readiness and will be revealed at the end of time.'

PRAYER:

O God, our Father, grant us
The faith which is sure and certain of what it believes;
The faith which is loyal to you in any situation.
The hope which will never despair;
The hope that no disappointment can quench;
The hope which in spite of failure will never give in.

The love which is always ready to forgive;
The love which is always eager to help;
The love which is always happier to give than to get.
And so grant that living in faith, in hope, in love, we may live like Jesus. *Amen.*

HYMNS: *All my hope on God is founded*
Lord of all hopefulness, Lord of all joy

31

'MANNERS MAKYTH MAN'

Aim: 'Good manners is the art of making those people easy with whom we converse. Whoever makes the fewest persons uneasy, is the best bred in the company.'

(*Swift*)

'Politeness goes far, yet costs nothing.'

(*Samuel Smiles*)

'Manners must adorn knowledge and smooth its way through the world.'

(*Chesterfield*)

Illustration:
Nobody knows how or when Christianity came to Britain. Some believe it was brought by Roman soldiers, others believe that it was probably brought by traders, and of course there is the haunting legend that it was brought to Glastonbury by Joseph of Arimathea.

What we can be certain about is that there was an established Church in Britain by the third century because there were British bishops present at the Council of Arles in 314.

In 409 the Roman legions were withdrawn from Britain, and the Island was invaded by the Saxons. Christianity was almost wiped out – except in those western parts of the land where the Celts maintained their independence.

Meanwhile, in far distant Rome, so the Venerable Bede tells us,

Pope Gregory the Great, whilst walking in the market place saw some boys put up for sale as slaves. He was so moved by their beauty, the lightness of their skin and fairness of their hair, that he asked which land they came from, and which people they belonged to. He was told that they came from Britain and that they were Angles. On hearing this, it is said that Gregory made his famous pun when he replied:

'Non Angli, sed angeli,' – 'Not Angles, but angels,' for 'they have the faces of angels and shall be made co-heirs with the angels in Heaven.'

This incident led Gregory, a few years later, to send Augustine to bring the Christian faith to England. Augustine landed in Kent in 597 and swiftly established his centre at Canterbury. He realized that the task which lay ahead was formidable and that any help would be more than welcome. When he learnt that there was an established church in Wales, he decided to ask the Welsh bishops to help him in his great endeavour. The Welsh bishops agreed to meet him at a place near Gloucester. On the eve of the meeting, the Welsh bishops held a discussion amongst themselves and agreed that if Augustine stood to greet them as they approached, they would listen sympathetically to what he had to say. On the other hand, if he remained seated as they approached, they would not cooperate.

In the event, Augustine did not stand, and the Welsh bishops did not cooperate, which meant that Augustine's work was made much more difficult and the conversion of the English long delayed.

READINGS:

St Matthew 20,25–28. '. . . Jesus called them to him and said, "You know that in the world, rulers lord it over their subjects, and their great men make them feel the weight of authority; but it shall not be so with you. Among you, whoever wants to be great must be your servant, and whoever would be first must be the willing slave of all – like the Son of Man; he did not come to be served, but to serve, and to surrender his life as a ransom for many."'

Philippians 2,5–8. 'Let your bearing towards one another arise out of your life in Christ Jesus. For the divine nature was his from the first; yet he did not think to snatch at equality with God, but made himself nothing, assuming the nature of a slave. Bearing the human likeness, revealed in human shape, he humbled himself, and in obedience accepted even death – death on a cross.'

PRAYER:

Take from us, O God,
All pride and vanity,
All boasting and forwardness,
And give us the true courage that shows itself by gentleness;
The true wisdom that shows itself by simplicity;
And the true power that shows itself by modesty;
Through Jesus Christ our Lord. *Amen.*

(*Charles Kingsley, 1819–75*)

HYMNS: *Rise up, O men of God*
Help us, O Lord, to learn

32

JUDGEMENT

Aim: 'Do not judge superficially, but be just in your judgements.'
(*St John 7,24*)

'One cool judgement is worth a thousand hasty councils. The thing to do is to supply light and not heat.
(*Woodrow Wilson – Speech in 1916*)

A distinguished judge of the High Court said after his retirement, 'There have been times without number that I have had to revise my opinion as cases have unfolded before me.' We must beware of hasty judgements!

Illustration:

The morning came, but my servant appeared not.

Doors were all open, the water was not drawn from the well; my servant had been out all night; my morning meal was not ready; my clothes were all lying unfolded.

As the hours passed by, my anger grew and I devised hard punishments for him. At last he came, late in the morning and bowed low.

I called out angrily, 'Go forth from my presence and never see my face again.'

He looked at me and remained silent and then said in a low, husky voice, 'My little daughter died last night.' And without another word, he went to his daily task.

(*Rabindranath Tagore, 1861–1941*)

READINGS:

Luke 6,37–38 and 41–42.

'Pass no judgement, and you will not be judged; do not condemn, and you will not be condemned; acquit, and you will be acquitted; give, and gifts will be given you. Good measure, pressed down, shaken together, and running over, will be poured into your lap; for whatever measure you deal out to others will be dealt to you in return.'

'Why do you look at the speck of sawdust in your brother's eye, with never a thought for the great plank in your own? How can you say to your brother, "My dear brother, let me take the speck out of your eye", when you are blind to the plank in your own? You hypocrite! First take the plank out of your own eye, and then you will see clearly to take the speck out of your brother's.'

PRAYER:

Help us, O God, at all times to act towards others as we would wish them to act towards us.
Help us,
To make the same allowances for others as we would wish them to make for us,
To be as sympathetic and understanding to others as we would wish them to be to us;
To encourage others as we would wish them to encourage us;
To help others as we would wish them to help us;
To be as just and fair to others as we would wish them to be to us;
To forgive others as we would wish them to forgive us.
Before we criticize others, help us to remember what it feels like to be criticized.
Before we find fault with others, help us to remember what it feels like to be found fault with.
Before we condemn others, help us to remember what it feels like to be condemned.

Help us at all times to be like Jesus,
Who went about doing good;
Who was among men as one who serves;
Who even on the Cross prayed that his enemies should be forgiven. *Amen.*

(*William Barclay*)

HYMNS: *Gracious Spirit, Holy Ghost*
Help us, O Lord, to learn

33

PRE-JUDGEMENT

Aim: Most of the difficulties we anticipate never materialize. We waste a lot of energy by jumping to wrong conclusions.

Illustration:
A motorist whilst travelling one wet wintry night along a lonely mountain road in mid-Wales had a puncture. In bad humour, he climbed out of his car and pulled on his heavy raincoat. He opened the boot and lifted out the spare wheel. He placed the special spanner for undoing the nuts alongside the wheel, and reached for the jack. To his horror it could not be found! Evidently, he had not replaced it, after he had last used it.

What was he to do? As he stood there with the rain beating down on him, he noticed a light far up on the hillside.

'Ah,' he thought to himself, 'a farm! They must surely have a jack which I can borrow.'

Without further delay, he made his way up the narrow pot-holed road towards the farm. As he went he began to imagine the reception he would probably get at the farm house, because, after all, it was getting very late.

'I shall knock on the door,' he thought, 'a yapping dog will charge down the passage, and the door will be opened by a suspicious and tired farmer. I shall explain to him that I have had a puncture on the main road, and have come without my jack, and would he kindly let me borrow his. He will probably mumble something about disturbing law abiding citizens at this time of night, grudgingly put on his raincoat, demand a cash deposit in case I do not return the jack, and reluctantly hand it over.'

Plodding on further, the motorist thought, 'It won't be as easy as that. The farmer will probably be carrying a gun, in case I am a thief and a robber, and will be very fierce with me. I shall have to use all my powers of persuasion, before he will lend it. In every probability, the farmer will be in bed when I knock on his door, and he will open his bedroom window and point his gun at me and order me off, and I shall have great difficulty in trying to prove that I am a respectable citizen who has had a puncture and all I want is to borrow his jack.'

By the time the motorist reached the farmhouse, he had worked himself into a towering rage. He hammered on the door with both fists and waited. Eventually the door slowly opened to reveal an elderly gentleman who gently said,

'Good evening! Please step inside out of the rain. Is there anything I can do to help?'

'No, there is not,' raved the motorist. 'I have just come to tell you that I would not borrow your jack under any circumstances.'

READING:

James 3,1–12. 'My brothers, not many of you should become teachers, for you may be certain that we who teach shall ourselves be judged with greater strictness. All of us often go wrong; the man who never says a wrong thing is a perfect character, able to bridle his whole being. If we put bits into horses' mouths to make them obey our will, we can direct their whole body. Or think of ships: large they may be, yet even when driven by strong gales they can be directed by a tiny rudder on whatever course the helmsman chooses. So with the tongue. It is a small member but it can make huge claims.

What a huge stack of timber can be set ablaze by the tiniest spark! And the tongue is in effect a fire. It represents among our members the world with all its wickedness; it pollutes our whole being; it keeps the wheel of our existence red-hot, and its flames are fed by hell. Beasts and birds of every kind, creatures that crawl on the ground or swim in the sea, can be subdued and have been subdued by mankind; but no man can subdue the tongue. It is an intractable evil, charged with deadly venom. We use it to sing the praises of our Lord and Father, and we use it to invoke curses upon our fellow-men who are made in God's likeness. Out of the same mouth come praises and curses. My brothers, this should not be so. Does a fountain gush with both fresh and brackish water from the same opening? Can a fig-tree, my brothers, yield olives, or a vine figs? No more does salt water yield fresh.'

PRAYER:

Go before us, O Lord, in all our doings with thy most gracious favour, and further us with thy continual help; that in all our works, begun, continued and ended in thee, we may glorify thy holy name, and finally by thy mercy obtain everlasting life: through Jesus Christ our Lord. *Amen.*

HYMNS: *God be in my head and in my understanding*
Love divine, all loves excelling

34

ANGER

Aim: 'Anger is momentary madness, so control your passion or it will control you.'

(*Horace – Epistles*)

'Anger blows out the lamp of the mind.'

(*Ingersoll*)

Illustration:
One day a snake crept into an old loft to escape the approaching winter weather. As it slid through a crack in the wall, its long sleek body grazed against a rusty file that had been left lying against the wall.

Instantly the snake whipped around and bit the thing that had dared to hurt it. And as it bit, so the file wounded its mouth, infuriating the snake more and more. In pain, it struck again and again.

In the morning, the farmer, coming to tidy the dark corners of his loft, found the file leaning against the wall; and by it lay the dead body of the snake.

(*Aesop*)

READING:

Romans 12,10–21. 'Love in all sincerity, loathing evil and clinging to the good. Let love for our brotherhood breed warmth of mutual affection. Give pride of place to one another in esteem.

With unflagging energy, in ardour of spirit, serve the Lord.

Let hope keep you joyful; in trouble stand firm; persist in prayer.

Contribute to the needs of God's people, and practise hospitality.

Call down blessings on your persecutors – blessings, not curses.

With the joyful be joyful, and mourn with the mourners.

Have equal regard for one another. Do not be haughty, but go about with humble folk. Do not keep thinking how wise you are.

Never pay back evil for evil. Let your aims be such as all men count honourable. If possible, so far as it lies with you, live at peace with all men. My dear friends, do not seek revenge, but leave a place for divine retribution; for there is a text which reads, "Justice is mine, says the Lord, I will repay." But there is another text: "If your enemy is hungry, feed him; if he is thirsty, give him a drink; by doing this you will heap live coals on his head." Do not let evil conquer you, but use good to defeat evil.'

PRAYER:

May the power of the Father govern us.
May the wisdom of the Son enlighten us.
May the operation of the Holy Spirit quicken us.
O God, we beseech thee:
Guard our souls;
Sustain our bodies;
Exalt our senses;
Direct our course;
Regulate our manners;
Bless our undertakings;
Fulfil our petitions;
Inspire us with holy thoughts;

Pardon what is past;
Rectify what is present;
Order what is to come;
And all for the sake of Jesus Christ
Our Lord and Saviour, who alone
Can make us perfect as he is perfect. *Amen.*

(*Lancelot Andrewes, 1555–1620*)

HYMNS: *Give me joy in my heart, keep me praising*
Lift up your heads, you mighty gates

35

ANIMAL RIGHTS

Aim: He prayeth best, who loveth best
All things both great and small;
For the dear God who loveth us,
He made and loveth all.

(*S. T. Coleridge, The Ancient Mariner*)

Illustration:

Many centuries ago the town council of San Pedro became very concerned at the number of cases being brought before the magistrates. At one of their meetings, one of the councillors suggested that a bell be hung in the market place, so that anyone who had a grievance to air could ring the bell, and declare his or her grievance to the assembled crowd. The Council agreed that this was an excellent idea, and had a bell erected.

Soon the bell was being rung regularly, and the townspeople whenever they heard it, responded by rushing out of their houses and their business premises, to hear what complaint was being uttered.

'Look at this wine I bought yesterday, from Juan the wine merchant. It tastes awful, and he won't replace it,' complained a citizen.

'My husband comes home from the tavern on Saturday nights and beats me and the children,' wept a distraught housewife.

'Unless you are wealthy and powerful, you cannot persuade the magistrates to listen to your case,' lamented a poor cobbler.

'My landlord has put up my rent again because he wants my house for his friend,' cried an old widow, 'and I just cannot meet his demands.'

Within a month San Pedro became one of the most law abiding and considerate towns in the whole of Spain. The bell was hardly ever rung, because people realized the acute embarrassment which awaited anyone who misbehaved. Time went by and the bell rope just rotted away. The local parish priest noticed that there was no bell rope, and decided to do something about it – just in case! He invited a few members of his congregation to accompany him into the countryside, where they collected bundles of long dry grasses. Back in the Church vestry they plaited the grasses into a long rope and attached it to the bell.

Early one wintry morning, some months later, the township was awakened by the clanging of the market bell. Everyone leapt out of their beds, threw on their clothes and headed for the market place, wondering what juicy scandal they were going to hear.

When they arrived, they were astonished to see an old and decrepit donkey tugging at the rope in an endeavour to eat it.

'It's old Sebastian's donkey!' somebody said. 'He died a month ago, since which time his ancient and beloved donkey has had to roam the streets looking for scraps. Evidently he has not met with much success lately! Look at his bones sticking out through his coat! He must be desperately hungry to try and eat the bell rope!'

The citizens of San Pedro hung their heads with shame as the truth dawned on them, that whereas they were all prepared to use the bell for human rights, they had failed to recognize the rights of an old animal in their midst.

From that day on the donkey was fed and given shelter during cold weather – and San Pedro became known, not only for its law abiding citizens but also for its care of the animals committed to its charge.

READING:

Psalm 104.

'Bless the Lord, my soul:
O Lord my God, thou art great indeed,
clothed in majesty and splendour,
and wrapped in a robe of light.
Thou hast spread out the heavens like a tent
and on their waters laid the beams of thy pavilion;
who takest the clouds for thy chariot,

riding on the wings of the wind;
who makest the winds thy messengers
and flames of fire thy servants;
thou didst fix the earth on its foundation
so that it can never be shaken;
the deep overspread it like a cloak
and the waters lay above the mountains.
At thy rebuke they ran,
at the sound of thy thunder they rushed away,
flowing over the hills,
pouring down into the valleys
to the place appointed for them.
Thou didst fix a boundary which they might not pass;
they shall not return to cover the earth.

Thou dost make springs break out in the gullies,
so that their water runs between the hills.
The wild beasts all drink from them,
the wild asses quench their thirst;
the birds of the air nest on their banks
and sing among the leaves.
From thy high pavilion thou dost water the hills;
the earth is enriched by thy provision.
Thou makest grass grow for the cattle
and green things for those who toil for man,
bringing bread out of the earth
and wine to gladden men's hearts,
oil to make their faces shine
and bread to sustain their strength.
The trees of the Lord are green and leafy,
the cedars of Lebanon which he planted;
the birds build their nests in them,
the stork makes her home in their tops.
High hills are the haunt of the mountain-goat,
and boulders a refuge for the rock-badger.

Thou hast made the moon to measure the year
and taught the sun where to set.
When thou makest darkness and it is night,
all the beasts of the forest come forth;
the young lions roar for prey,
seeking their food from God.
When thou makest the sun rise, they slink away
and go to rest in their lairs;

but man comes out to his work
and to his labours until evening.
Countless are the things thou hast made, O Lord.
Thou hast made all by thy wisdom;
and the earth is full of thy creatures,
beasts great and small.
Here is the great immeasurable sea,
in which move creatures beyond number.
Here ships sail to and fro,
here is Leviathan whom thou has made thy plaything.

All of them look expectantly to thee
to give them their food at the proper time;
what thou givest them they gather up;
when thou openest thy hand, they eat their fill.
Then thou hidest thy face, and they are restless and troubled;
when thou takest away their breath, they fail
(and they return to the dust from which they came);
but when thou breathest into them, they recover;
thou givest new life to the earth.

May the glory of the Lord stand for ever
and may he rejoice in his works!
When he looks at the earth, it quakes;
when he touches the hills, they pour forth smoke.

I will sing to the Lord as long as I live,
all my life I will sing psalms to my God.
May my meditation please the Lord,
as I show my joy in him!
Away with all sinners from the earth
and may the wicked be no more!

Bless the Lord, my soul

O praise the Lord.'

To all the humble beasts there be,
To all the birds on land and sea,
Great Spirit! sweet protection give,
That free and happy they may live!

And to our hearts the rapture bring
Of love for every living thing;
Make of us all one kin, and bless
Our ways with Christ's own gentleness! (*John Galsworthy*)

Hi! handsome hunting man,
Fire your little gun.
Bang! Now the animal
Is dead and dumb and done.
Nevermore to peep again, creep again, leap again,
Eat or sleep or drink again. Oh, what fun!

(*Walter De La Mare*)

I think I could turn and live with animals, they're so placid and self contain'd,
I stand and look at them long and long.
They do not sweat and whine about their condition,
They do not lie awake in the dark and weep for their sins,
They do not make me sick discussing their duty to God.
Not one is dissatisfied – not one is demented with the mania of owning things,
Not one kneels to another, nor to his kind – that lived thousands of years ago;
Not one is respectable or unhappy over the whole earth.

(*Walt Whitman*)

PRAYERS:

O God, who hast made all the earth and every creature that dwells therein: Help us, we pray thee, to treat with compassion the living creatures entrusted to our care, that they may not suffer from our neglect nor become the victims of any cruelty; and grant that in caring for them we may find a deeper understanding of thy love and creation; through Jesus Christ our Lord. *Amen.*

Hear our humble prayer, O God, for our friends the animals, Thy creatures. We pray especially for all that are suffering in any way; for the overworked and underfed, the hunted, lost or hungry; for all in captivity or ill treated, and for those that must be put to death.

We entreat for them thy mercy and pity; and for those who deal with them we ask a heart of compassion, gentle hands and kindly words.

Make us all to be true friends to animals and so more worthy followers of our merciful Saviour Jesus Christ. *Amen.*

(*Source uncertain*)

HYMNS: *All things which live below the sky*
All creatures of our God and King

36

THE GOD OF THE UNIVERSE IS ALSO THE GOD OF THE DETAIL

Aim: The scientist has a faith . . . which is reflected in the fact that he would never consider that an experiment begun on Wednesday would yield entirely different results from one undertaken on a Friday. He believes in the orderliness of the universe. He stakes his shirt on his faith that everything happens in such a reasonable and well ordered fashion that the same experiment will give the same result . . . If the contents of our universe did not behave in so regular and predictable a fashion no real scientific research would be possible.

(*Robert Pilkington, World Without End*)

Illustration:

I have just come across some physiological facts. They are given as being true of the average woman, but I suppose that in general they will also be true of a man. The average woman owns 750 moveable muscles, 500 of which work in pairs. Her skin covers an area of 20 square feet. 'In any piece of her skin the size of a postage stamp there are four yards of nerves, a hundred sweat glands, fifteen oil glands, a yard of blood vessels, and three million assorted cells!' When you think of that, you can only say that in truth we are fearfully and wonderfully made (*Psalm 139.14*).

Now this is what we might call God working in a square inch; this tells us of the detailed marvel of creation; this is seeing God in the infinitesimally small things.

But then we go on to the other end of the scale, and we look at the universe. The astronomers measure the distance that stars are away in light years. A light year is the distance that light travels in a year. Light travels 186,000 miles per second. Therefore in one year light travels 186,000 multiplied by 60 for minutes, multiplied by 60 for hours, multiplied by 24 for days, multiplied by 365 for years.

Now the *nearest* star in the heavens is Alpha Centauri, which is four-and-one-third light years away. (That is to say, the nearest star to the earth is $186{,}000 \times 60 \times 60 \times 24 \times 365 \times 4\frac{1}{3}$ miles away.) The Pole Star is four hundred light years away. (That is to say, its distance from the earth is $186{,}000 \times 60 \times 60 \times 24 \times 365 \times 400$ miles.)

Put this another way. The light we see shining from the Pole Star left that star just about when Shakespeare was writing his plays, when the Authorised Version of the Bible was being written, and has been travelling ever since at 186,000 miles per second to get here. And when we think of that, we can say with far more amazement than ever the Psalmist could, 'When I look at the heavens, the work of thy fingers, the moon and the stars which thou hast established; what is man that thou art mindful of him, and the son of man that thou dost care for him?' (*Psalm 8,3–4*).

The point about all this is that we see God in two ways. First, we see in God *the most detailed care*. Nothing is too small for God. God's love of detail can be seen in the delicate tracery of every snowflake. The very structure of the universe shows us a God for whose care nothing is too small. We need never fear that, as far as God is concerned, we are lost in the mass. The very form of the universe makes it easy to believe in a God whose love is over every creature whom his hands has made.

Secondly, we see a God of *infinite power*. Nothing is too great to be beyond the control of God. The immensities of the universe obey the laws of the universe just as much as the atom or the molecule do. Just as the issues of the individual life are in the hands of God, so are the issues of the universe.

(*William Barclay, 'In the Hands of God', Collins Fount Paperbacks*)

There are millions and millions of worlds below and above
ours,
Man's mind is tired of this great search,
It cannot reach the end of his vastness.
How can the Infinite be reduced to the finite?
All attempts to describe Him are futile
He alone knows how great He is.
None knoweth the Lord's beginning nor His end.

(*Guru Nanah, Sikh*)

READING:

Psalm 139,1–18 and 23,24.

'Lord, thou hast examined me and knowest me.
Thou knowest all, whether I sit down or rise up;
thou hast discerned my thoughts from afar.
Thou hast traced my journey and my resting places,
and art familiar with all my paths.
For there is not a word on my tongue
but thou, Lord, knowest them all.
Thou hast kept close guard before me and behind
and hast spread thy hand over me.

Such knowledge is beyond my understanding,
  so high that I cannot reach it.
Where can I escape from thy spirit?
  Where can I flee from thy presence?
If I climb up to heaven, thou art there;
if I make my bed in Sheol, again I find thee.
If I take my flight to the frontiers of the morning
or dwell at the limits of the western sea,
even there thy hand will meet me
  and thy right hand will hold me fast.
If I say, "Surely darkness will steal over me,
  night will close around me".
darkness is no darkness for thee
  and night is luminous as day;
  to thee both dark and light are one.

Thou it was who didst fashion my inward parts;
thou didst knit me together in my mother's womb.
I will praise thee, for thou dost fill me with awe;
wonderful thou art, and wonderful thy works.
Thou knowest me through and through:
  my body is no mystery to thee,
how I was secretly kneaded into shape
  and patterned in the depths of the earth.
Thou didst see my limbs unformed in the womb,
  and in thy book they are all recorded;
  day by day they were fashioned,
  not one of them was late in growing.
How did I find thy thoughts, O God,
  how inexhaustible their themes!
Can I count them? They outnumber the grains of sand;
to finish the count, my years must equal thine . . .

Examine me, O God, and know my thoughts;
  test me, and understand my misgivings.
Watch lest I follow any path that grieves thee;
  guide me in the ancient ways.'

PRAYER:

Lord of infinite greatness, who hast ordered and adorned in equal perfection all that thou hast made; who hast set in glorious array the eternal heavens, and yet dost paint the lily that abideth but a day: Give us courage to attempt great things in thy Name, and equal faithfulness to do the small; to thy sole honour and glory; through Jesus Christ Our Lord. *Amen.*

HYMNS: *Lord of beauty, thine the splendour*
For the beauty of the earth

37

GOD

Aim: Where is the emphasis in the Creed? Is it '*I* believe in God'. Or is it 'I believe in *God*?' There is no doubt where the answer of all wholesome religion lies . . . the thing that is important is that there is a God to believe in.

(*William Temple*)

Is our concept of God too small? Are we only prepared to believe in a God who will fit our own ideas of what he should be?

Illustration:
There was a man who did not believe in God. Late one stormy winter's night, he was walking along a cliff-top pathway, when suddenly a strong gust of wind caused him to lose his balance. He slipped on the wet grass and slid down the slope and over the edge. As he fell his outstretched hands managed to grasp hold of a protruding rock. There he hung, with his feet dangling in space, and the waves crashing on the jagged rocks far below. In his desperate plight he shouted,

'Is there anyone there? Is there anyone there?'

To his joy and surprise he heard a calm voice answering,

'Yes, *I* am here!'

'Please help me,' pleaded the man, 'if you do, I will believe in you for the rest of my life.'

'Of course I will help you,' came the reply, 'just let go of your hold.'

The man remained silent for a moment or so, and then shouted,

'Is there anyone else there?'

READINGS:

St John 1,1–14. 'When all things began, the Word already was. The Word dwelt with God, and what God was, the Word was.

The Word, then, was with God at the beginning, and through him all things came to be; no single thing was created without him. All that came to be was alive with his life, and that life was the light of men. The light shines on in the dark, and the darkness has never quenched it.

There appeared a man named John, sent from God; he came as a witness to testify to the light, that all might become believers through him. He was not himself the light; he came to bear witness to the light. The real light which enlightens every man was even then coming into the world.

He was in the world; but the world, though it owed its being to him, did not recognize him. He entered his own realm, and his own would not receive him. But to all who did receive him, to those who have yielded him their allegiance, he gave the right to become children of God, not born of any human stock, or by the fleshly desire of a human father, but the offspring of God himself. So the Word became flesh; he came to dwell among us, and we saw his glory, such glory as befits the Father's only Son, full of grace and truth.'

1 John 4,7–12. 'Dear friends, let us love one another, because love is from God. Everyone who loves is a child of God and knows God, but the unloving know nothing of God. For God is love; and his love was disclosed to us in this, that he sent his only Son into the world to bring us life. The love I speak of is not our love for God, but the love he showed to us in sending his Son as the remedy for the defilement of our sins. If God thus loved us, dear friends, we in turn are bound to love one another. Though God has never been seen by any man, God himself dwells in us if we love one another; his love is brought to perfection within us.'

PRAYER:

Lord, increase our faith, that feeling towards thee as children we may trust where we cannot see, and hope where all seems doubtful, ever looking unto thee as our Father that ordereth all things well, and patiently doing the work thou hast given us to do; according to the word of thy Son, Jesus Christ our Lord. *Amen.*

(*George Dawson 1821–1870*)

HYMNS: *Have faith in God, my heart*
Fill thou my life, O Lord my God

38

TIME

Aim: If we are to be careful custodians of our time, we must be careful not to slip into the pattern of 'busily doing nothing, nothing the whole day through'.

Illustration:

Upstairs and Downstairs

Owl's house had an upstairs and a downstairs.
The staircase had twenty steps.
Some of the time Owl was upstairs in his bedroom.
At other times Owl was downstairs in his living room.
When Owl was downstairs he said,
'I wonder how my upstairs is?'
When Owl was upstairs, he said,
'I wonder how my downstairs is doing?
I am always missing one place or the other.
There must be a way,' said Owl,
'to be upstairs and to be downstairs at the same time.
Perhaps if I run very very fast, I can be
in both places at once.'
Owl ran up the stairs.
'I am up,' he said.
Owl ran down the stairs.
'I am down,' he said.
Owl ran up and down the stairs faster and faster.
'Owl' he cried. 'Are you downstairs?'
There was no answer.
'No,' said Owl. 'I am not downstairs because I am upstairs.
I am not running fast enough.'
'Owl' he shouted. 'Are you upstairs?'
There was no answer.
'No,' said Owl. 'I am not upstairs because I am downstairs.
I must run even faster.
Faster, faster, faster!' cried Owl.
Owl ran upstairs and downstairs all evening.
But he could not be in both places at once.
'When I am up,' said Owl,
'I am not down. When I am down, I am not up.
All I am is very tired!'

Owl sat down to rest. He sat on the tenth step
Because it was a place that was right in the middle.

(*Owl at Home by Arnold Lobel,
World's Work Ltd, The Windmill Press,
Kingswood, Tadworth, Surrey*)

READING:

Ecclesiastes 3,1–8. 'For everything its season, and for every activity under heaven its time:

a time to be born and a time to die;
a time to plant and a time to uproot;
a time to kill and a time to heal;
a time to pull down and a time to build up;
a time to weep and a time to laugh;
a time for mourning and a time for dancing;
a time to scatter stones and a time to gather them;
a time to embrace and a time to refrain from embracing;
a time to seek and a time to lose;
a time to keep and a time to throw away;
a time to tear and a time to mend;
a time for silence and a time for speech;
a time to love and a time to hate;
a time for war and a time for peace.'

PRAYER:

I will not hurry through this day!
Lord, I will listen by the way,
To humming bees and singing birds,
To speaking trees and friendly words;
And for the moments in between
Seek glimpses of thy great Unseen.

I will not hurry through this day;
I will take time to think and pray;
I will look up into the sky,
Where fleecy clouds and swallows fly:
And somewhere in the day, may be
I will catch whispers, Lord, from thee.

(*Ralph Spaulding Cushman, Prayers for Children
and Young People, Hodder & Stoughton*)

Lord, help me to remember that all time belongs to you, and that I am responsible to you for the use of it. Help me neither to waste time nor be so obsessed with saving it that I become the slave of time and lose my sense of proportion and values.

Lord, teach me to use my time to your glory, creatively, re-creatively, in that rhythm of involvement in the world and withdrawal from the world which is your will for me. Save me from running away from the world into self-centred religiosity. *Amen*.

HYMNS: *Awake, my soul, and with the sun*
Forth in thy name, O Lord, I go

39

REMEMBRANCE SUNDAY

Aim: To wage war for an 'unjust' cause is evil. To wage war for a 'just' cause is not to wage a 'just' war, but simply to engage oneself in the lesser of two evils. War is an obscene form of human activity.

Illustration:

The Times *of August 28, 1916*

The offensive at High Wood in the battlefield of the Somme. The *Times* correspondent wrote:

'In the course of my life I have seen many gigantic things, like typhoons and prairie fires and forest fires, and most of the great volcanoes, of the world, and some battles, and the fall of Antwerp. But, merely as a spectacle, for the splendour and the power of it, I doubt if anything ever resembled what went on then for the next twenty minutes . . .

How many guns we had at work I do not know, and I could not tell if I knew. Hundreds – thousands – millions – I do not know. But they began all at once, breaking suddenly on the sunlit silence. In ten seconds hundreds of shells had plunged upon that one devoted spot of earth. In twenty seconds, it seemed as if there must have been thousands of hurricanes, whirlwinds, thunderstorms, and gigantic conflagrations – bring them all together and concentrate them all in a ring of a few acres, and you will have only a suggestion of what went on immediately before our eyes . . .

As for the ground where the shots fell, it simply was not. Rent and torn in every direction, it heaved itself into the air, not in spurts or bursts, but universally in one great dust storm. There was no ground, no trench, no brown earth, or green; nothing but chaos, swirling and incredible; and then the smoke grew, and blotted even chaos out.'

For an advance of 1000 yards that day 60,000 British lives were lost.

This happened on one morning, in one place in one hour.

We are invited today to contemplate at least *two* things: firstly, sadness, sympathy, and respect for those who were caught up in the tragedy of war; secondly, shame and horror at what we have done to each other.

We are called to be builders of the future. We are called to be co-workers with God in the building of the City of God on this earth. Through our actions, concrete and creative, we set about to change the patterns of this world that have made, and perhaps still make for hatred and resentment and poverty and unemployment and war and death. We are not just to *pray* for the *coming* of the City of God and to contemplate the implications of its arrival – but actually to take a significant part in the building of the City of God.

(*Dr J. H. Shepherd*)

'Ours is a world of nuclear giants and ethical infants. We know more about war than we know about living. We have grasped the mystery of the atom and rejected the "Sermon on the Mount".'

(*General Omar Bradley*)

READING:

Micah 4,2–4.

'Come, let us climb up on to the mountain of the Lord,
to the house of the God of Jacob,
that he may teach us his ways
and we may walk in his paths.'
For instruction issues from Zion,
and out of Jerusalem comes the word of the Lord;
he will be judge between many peoples
and arbiter among mighty nations afar.
They shall beat their swords into mattocks
and their spears into pruning-knives;
nation shall not lift sword against nation

nor ever again be trained for war,
and each man shall dwell under his own vine,
under his own fig-tree, undisturbed.
For the Lord of Hosts himself has spoken.'

PRAYER:

Eternal God, in whose perfect kingdom no sword is drawn but the sword of righteousness, and no strength known but the strength of love: We pray thee so mightily to shed and spread abroad thy Spirit, that all peoples and ranks may be gathered under one banner, of the Prince of Peace; as children of one God and Father of all, to whom be dominion and glory now and for ever. *Amen.*

HYMNS: *For the healing of the nations*
Almighty Father, who for us thy Son didst give

40

CHRISTMAS

Aim: So long as one does not become simple like a child, one does not get divine illumination. Forget all the worldly knowledge that thou hast acquired and become as a child, and then wilt thou get the divine wisdom.

(*Ramakrishna. Hindu*)

'"I tell you, whoever does not accept the kingdom of God like a child will never enter it." And he put his hands upon them, and blessed them.'

(*Mark 10, 15 & 16*)

Illustration:
The congregation of St Peter's Church decided to invest in a new set of figures for the Christmas crib. The old ones were faded and damaged with a leg missing here, and an arm or two missing there. During the course of the year, they held a bazaar and a number of

coffee mornings until the desired sum of money was accumulated and a local sculptor was commissioned to make the figures.

On the day before Christmas, the crib was set up and the figures placed in their appropriate places. There was even an innkeeper holding a lamp behind Mary so that the shepherds might get a better view of the infant lying on a pile of fresh straw.

Early on Christmas Day, the Vicar arrived to take the morning service. He could not resist the temptation of taking a quick look at the nativity scene as he made his way to the vestry. As he did so, he stopped suddenly in his tracks and took a swift breath. The figure of the baby Jesus was missing! He could not believe his eyes. Who on earth would do such a thing? He looked everywhere just in case someone may have moved it. But the baby Jesus could nowhere be found. As the parishioners arrived, they all noticed that the central figure was missing, and there was much muttering and shaking of heads.

After the service, the Vicar was walking along the pavement to the vicarage when he was nearly knocked over by an eight year old boy in a brand new pedal car.

'Careful!' smiled the Vicar, 'otherwise you will get arrested for careless driving.'

Suddenly the smile left his face, for there on the seat of the pedal car, alongside the driver, was the missing figure.

'What on earth are you doing with that figure of Jesus?' exclaimed the Vicar. 'You must have taken it from the Church! That is a very wrong thing to do. What do you have to say for yourself?'

The little boy hung his head and then very quietly said,

'I desperately wanted Santa Claus to bring me a pedal car for Christmas so I prayed hard for it. I even went so far as to promise Jesus that if he would grant my request, I would take him for a ride. So that is what I am doing.'

READINGS:

St Luke 2,1–14. 'In those days a decree was issued by the Emperor Augustus for a general registration throughout the Roman world. This was the first registration of its kind; it took place when Quirinius was governor of Syria. For this purpose everyone made his way to his own town; and so Joseph went up to Judaea from the town of Nazareth in Galilee, to be registered at the city of David, called Bethlehem, because he was of the house of David by descent; and with him went Mary who was betrothed to him. She was pregnant, and while they were there the time came for her child to be born, and she gave birth to a son, her first-born. She wrapped him round, and laid him in a manger, because there was no room for them to lodge in the house.

Now in this same district there were shepherds out in the fields, keeping watch through the night over their flock, when suddenly there stood before them an angel of the Lord, and the splendour of the Lord shone round them. They were terror-struck, but the angel said, "Do not be afraid; I have good news for you: there is great joy coming to the whole people. Today in the city of David a deliverer has been born to you – the Messiah, the Lord. And this is your sign: you will find a baby lying all wrapped up, in a manger." All at once there was with the angel a great company of the heavenly host, singing the praises of God:

"Glory to God in highest heaven,
And on earth his peace for men on whom his favour rests."'

St Matthew 2,1–12.

Philippians 2,1–11.

PRAYERS:

Heavenly Father, we thank thee for all thy love to us. We remember again at this Christmas time the gift of the Lord Jesus and his birth at Bethlehem. We pray that we may welcome him with gladness, and that there may always be room for him both in our hearts and in our homes. We ask it in his name, who is our Saviour and our Friend. *Amen.*

May the humility of the shepherds, the perseverance of the Wise Men, the joy of the angels, and the peace of the Christ-child be God's gifts to you this Christmas time, and always.

HYMNS: *O little town of Bethlehem*
Once in royal David's city

41

EASTER (I)

Aim: 'We come from God – and we go to God.'

Illustration:
The Venerable Bede (673–735) in his *Ecclesiastical History of the English Nation* tells us what happened immediately after St Paulinus had declared the Christian Gospel to Edwin King of Northumbria and his Council of elder statesmen. The King turned to his Council and asked each one separately, what his thoughts were regarding this new religion. One of the elders replied,

'Up until now, O King, it seems to me, that our understanding of life can be likened to the swift flight of a sparrow through the room wherein you sit at supper in winter, with your commanders and ministers, and a good fire in the midst, whilst the storms of rain and snow prevail outside. The sparrow, I say, flying in at one door, and immediately out at another, whilst he is within, is safe from the wintry storm; but after a short space inside the light and warmth of the room, vanishes once again into the darkness from which he had emerged. So this life of man appears for a short space. We emerge from darkness and return to darkness. If, therefore, this new teaching, sheds light on what it is to be, it seems worth following.'

John Bunyan (1628–88) writing almost a thousand years later in his book *The Pilgrim's Progress* because of his Christian conviction was able to describe the death of Mr Valiant for Truth thus:

'Then said he, I am going to my Fathers, and though with great difficulty I am got hither, yet now I do not repent me of all the trouble I have been at to arrive where I am. My Sword, I give to him that shall succeed me in my pilgrimage, and my Courage and Skill to him that can get it. My marks and scars I carry with me, to be a witness for me that I have fought His battles who now will be my Rewarder.'

When the day that he must go hence was come, many accompanied him to the river side, into which, as he went, he said, 'Death, where is thy sting?' And as he went down deeper, he said, 'Grave where is thy victory?' So he passed over and the trumpets sounded for him on the other side.

READING:

(The unbeliever says)

'Our life is short and tedious, and in the death of a man there is no remedy; neither was there any man known to have returned from the grave. For we were born at all adventure, and we shall be hereafter as though we had never been; for the breath in our nostrils is as smoke, and a little spark in the moving of our hearts, which being extinguished, our body shall be turned into ashes, and our spirits shall vanish as the soft air, and our name shall be forgotten in time, and no man shall have our works in remembrance, and our life shall pass away as the trace of a cloud, and shall be dispersed as a mist that is driven away with the beams of the sun, and overcome with the heat thereof.

For our time is a very shadow that passeth away, and after our end there is no returning: for it is fast sealed, so that no man cometh again.'

(*Wisdom of Solomon 11,1–6*)

(The believer can say)
'But the souls of the righteous are in the hand of God,
And there shall no torment touch them.
In the sight of fools they seem to die;
And their departure is taken for misery,
And their going from us to be utter destruction;
But they are in peace.
For though they be punished in the sight of man,
Yet is their hope full of immortality.
And having been a little chastised, they shall be greatly rewarded:
For God proved them, and found them worthy for himself.
As gold in the furnace hath he proved them,
And received them as a burnt offering.
And in the time of their visitation they shall shine,
And run to and fro like sparks among the stubble.
They shall judge the nations, and have dominion over the people,
And the Lord shall reign over them for ever.
They that put their trust in him shall understand the truth:
And such as be faithful shall abide with him in love:
For grace and mercy are to his saints,
And he hath care for his elect.'

(*Wisdom of Solomon 3,1–9*)

or

1 Corinthians 15,20–end.

PRAYER:

Lord Jesus, you came into this world that man might have life and have it more abundantly. May your Spirit ever dwell in this place, and be to those who move therein, the Way, the Truth and the Life. *Amen.*

HYMNS: *Jesus Christ is risen today*
Light's glittering morn

42

EASTER (II)

Aim: Just as the frog climbs up from a life under water to a new life in the fresh air *without ceasing to be the same creature*, so human beings that 'die' climb up to a higher world of life without ceasing to be the same living souls. We cannot hope to understand what the new life is like while we ourselves are (so to speak) still in the pond, but we can see from the example of the tadpole becoming a frog that death makes no difference to the *continuity of life*. That is the great message of the Christian Faith about Death.

Illustration:
A whole colony of tadpoles lived at the bottom of a murky little pond, full of mud and weeds. They thought that their gloomy little pond was the whole world, though they often wondered what was up through the 'sky' (as they called it). Every now and then a sad thing happened. One of their number would 'die' (or 'grow legs' as they expressed it) and disappear up through the 'sky', never to be seen again. The tadpoles were very puzzled and worried about it. They thought he had gone out of existence altogether, because they could not imagine any other world but their little, gloomy pond.

One day a frog came tumbling back into the pond. The tadpoles were terrified because they thought they were seeing a 'ghost'; but in a moment or two they recognized him as one of their number who had 'died' (or 'grown legs') only a day or two before. The frog tried to describe to them the glorious upper world into which he had climbed; he tried to describe the loveliness of trees and meadows and fresh air and glorious sunshine. But all in vain. How can you describe trees and air and sunshine to creatures that only know weeds and water and gloom? But what he *could* explain was that he was not dead after all, but had merely climbed up to a richer and more glorious world of life.

(*J. G. Williams*)

READINGS:

St John 20,10–29. 'So the disciples went home again; but Mary stood at the tomb outside, weeping. As she wept, she peered into the tomb; and she saw two angels in white sitting there, one at the head, and one at the feet, where the body of Jesus had lain. They said to her, "Why are you weeping?" She answered, "They have taken my Lord away, and I do not know where they have laid him." With these words she turned round and saw Jesus standing there, but did not recognize him. Jesus said to her, "Why are you weeping? Who is it you are looking for?" Thinking it was the gardener, she said, "If it is you, sir, who removed him, tell me where you have laid him, and I will take him away." Jesus said, "Mary." She turned to him and said, "Rabbuni!" (which is Hebrew for "My Master"). Jesus said, "Do not cling to me, for I have not yet ascended to the Father. But go to my brothers, and tell them that I am now ascending to my Father and your Father, my God and your God." Mary of Magdala went to the disciples with her news: "I have seen the Lord," she said, and gave them his message.

Late that Sunday evening, when the disciples were together behind locked doors, for fear of the Jews, Jesus came and stood among them. "Peace be with you," he said, and then showed them his hands and his side. So when the disciples saw the Lord, they were filled with joy. Jesus repeated, "Peace be with you", and then said, "As the Father sent me, so I send you." He then breathed on them, saying, "Receive the Holy Spirit! If you forgive any man's sins, they stand forgiven; if you pronounce them unforgiven, unforgiven they remain."

One of the Twelve, Thomas, that is "the Twin", was not with the rest when Jesus came. So the disciples told him, "We have seen the Lord." He said, "Unless I see the mark of the nails on his hands, unless I put my finger into the place where the nails were, and my hand into his side, I will not believe it."

A week later his disciples were again in the room, and

Thomas was with them. Although the doors were locked, Jesus came and stood among them, saying, "Peace be with you." Then he said to Thomas, "Reach your finger here: see my hands; reach your hand here and put it into my side; be unbelieving no longer, but believe." Thomas said, "My Lord and my God." Jesus said, "Because you have seen me you have found faith. Happy are they who never saw me and yet have found faith."

1 Corinthians 15,35–57.

PRAYERS:

Bring us, O Lord God, at our last awakening into the house and gate of heaven, to enter into that gate and dwell in that house, where there shall be no darkness nor dazzling, but one equal light; no noise nor silence, but one equal music; no fears nor hopes, but one equal possession; no ends nor beginnings, but one equal eternity; in the habitations of thy glory and dominion world without end. *Amen.*

(*John Donne*)

O God we thank you for the message of Easter Day:
We thank you that Jesus conquered death and rose from the grave;
We thank you that he is alive for ever more;
We thank you that he is with us always even to the end of the world,
We thank you for letting us know through Jesus that death is not the end but simply the entrance through which we enter Heaven. *Amen.*

HYMNS: *Thine be the glory, risen conquering Son*
I danced in the morning

43

EASTER (III)

Aim: There is nothing in the world of which I feel so certain. I have no idea what it will be like, and I am glad that I have not, as I am sure it would be wrong. I do not want it for myself as mere continuance, but I want it for my understanding of life. And moreover 'God is love' appears to me nonsense in view of the world He has made, if there is no other.

(*William Temple*)

'Death is not extinguishing the light, it is only putting out the lamp because the dawn has come.'

(*Tagore*)

Illustration:
John, like his father before him, was an extremely fine cricketer. John's father never missed a game in which his son played. During a game he clapped every run and listened with extreme interest to all the comments uttered around him. After every game, he and John discussed each ball and each stroke in minute detail. But John's father never actually saw John play, because John's father was blind. One day John's father died. John had been chosen to play in an important match the day after, and everyone expected that with such a heavy loss on his mind, he would not be up to his usual form. They were mistaken. He played brilliantly. At last he came out after a magnificent innings, and a close friend said to him,

'How could you play so well at a time like this?'

John replied, 'Because that was the first time my father has ever seen me play.'

READING:

St John 14,1–6. 'Set your troubled hearts at rest. Trust in God always; trust also in me. There are many dwelling-places in my Father's house; if it were not so I should have told you; for I am going there on purpose to prepare a place for you. And if I go and prepare a place for you, I shall come again and receive you to myself, so that where I am you may be also; and my way there is known to you. Thomas said, "Lord, we do not know where you are going, so how can we know the way?" Jesus replied, "I am the way; I am the truth and I am life; no one comes to the Father except by me."'

PRAYER:

We give back, to you, O God, those whom you gave us. You did not lose them when you gave them to us, and we do not lose them by their return to you. Your Son has taught us that life is eternal and love cannot die. So death is only an horizon, and an horizon is only the limit of our sight. Open our eyes to see more clearly, and draw us closer to you that we may know that we are nearer to our loved ones, who are with you. You have told us that you are preparing a place for us: prepare us also for that happy place, that where you are we may also be always, O dear Lord of life and death.

(*William Penn, 1644–1718*)

HYMNS: *Jesus lives! thy terrors now*
Ye choirs of new Jerusalem